HOW TO BE
Funny

JON MACKS

Simon & Schuster
New York London Toronto Sydney Singapore

SIMON & SCHUSTER
Rockefeller Center
1230 Avenue of the Americas
New York, NY 10020

For information regarding special discounts for bulk purchases,
please contact Simon & Schuster Special Sales at 1-800-456-6798
or business@simonandschuster.com

Designed by Laura Lindgren

Manufactured in the United States of America

10 9 8 7 6 5 4 3 2 1

Library of Congress Cataloging-in-Publication Data

Macks, Jon.
    How to be funny / Jon Macks.
        p. cm.
    1. Wit and humor—History and criticism. I. Title.
    PN6147.M124 2003
    817.009—dc21   2003050665

ISBN 0-7432-0472-7

To Julie, Daniel, Samantha, and Ricky

Acknowledgments

To David Rosenthal, Marysue Rucci, Tara Parsons, and all the people at Simon & Schuster who inspired and guided me through this.

To Jay Leno, the best boss anyone could have and the funniest person I have ever known.

To James Carville, who came up with the idea for this book, and to Mary Matalin, for her words of encouragement throughout this process.

To Billy Crystal, Steve Martin, Whoopi Goldberg, David Steinberg, Gil Cates, Don Mischer, Lou Horvitz, Michael Seligman, Jeff Margolis, Gary Smith, George Schlatter, Henry Winkler, Michael Levitt, Pat Lee, John Moffitt, Bruce Vilanch, Tom Bergeron, and Jay Redack, all of whom gave me a start in comedy writing or a break along the way.

To all the people, some of whom are mentioned above, who contributed their wisdom and humor to this book: Garry Shandling, Conan O'Brien, Rita Rudner, Arsenio Hall, Carrie Fisher, Buz Kohan, Paul Begala, Bob Ellison, Stefanie Wilder, Gilbert Gottfried, Eddie Driscoll, Dave Barry, Paul Harris, Jeffrey Ross, and Andy Breckman.

To Dave Boone and Bob O'Donnell for their friendship and support.

To all the writers at *The Tonight Show* and *Hollywood Squares* who show the world every day what funny really is.

To Jack Dytman, Bob Myman, Les Abell, and Mike Klein, who handle the behind the scenes for Wild Bronco Productions.

To the makers of Valtrex.

To my parents, Albert and Sylvia, my brother, Adam, his wife, Susan, and my nephew, Jeremy.

To my new baseball team, the Cobras. For those who follow this, this is my sixth team in ten years and I'm not being traded because I'm good.

To Bill Kernochan, Bob Benton, and Mike Justice, who step in and cover for me when I blow off my sports coaching obligations.

To the makers of Bombay Sapphire gin.

To Josh, my personal trainer, who in two years has turned a 165-pound weakling into a 164-pound weakling.

To Senator Herb Kohl, Senator Tom Daschle, and Senator John Kerry, who are great public servants and even better human beings.

To the makers of the EPT home pregnancy test.

To the Agoura Cyclones and the Agoura Bronco AA's.

To Fang and Bridget, Denise, Dennis, Katie and Kara, Bob and Beth, Rob and Kaye, whom I mention by name so they will actually buy this book.

And finally, to that special person out there who wasn't mentioned by name, but you know who you are and what you've done for me. Or is it what you've done *to* me?

HOW TO BE
Funny

1.

Introduction

This book has one aim—to teach you how to be funny in everyday life. It won't help you become a standup comic, and it won't help you become a comedy writer. It won't help you repeat other people's jokes, and it definitely won't increase your chances of recovering the $20,000 you lost in WorldCom last year.

But if you read this book from front to back, follow the advice, and work at being funny, you will learn to use humor to: improve your public speaking; end an argument; avoid getting beaten up; get a raise at work; make people think you're smart. You will see that being funny can make you more popular, enable you to pass the time in prison without being violated by large, angry men (especially useful for you CEO's out there), and help you get selected as a contestant on a game show because the producers look for amusing extroverts on these shows, not Harry Potter–obsessed introverts. In short, this book can help you ridicule and diminish your enemies, handle your kids, and deal with idiots in every-day situations; it will enable you to make a point, and ruin a rival's big moment—and all of this for only $12.

Historically the male book buyer is the hardest to entice. (Unless the book has a lot of pictures and a centerfold.) So if the above-mentioned reasons don't inspire you, how about the fact that this book will help improve your sex life? If there is one thing that is certain in life, it's that the number-one trait women look for in deciding whether to have sex with someone they just met is a sense of humor. So if you have a big expense account, a six figure income, *plus* a sense of humor, you've got it made.

One thing to remember as you begin your journey to funny: A lot of this book is repetitive. A lot of the advice from the pros is repetitive. This is not because I get paid by the word. It's so you will realize that to be funny, there are a few basic fundamentals of comedy that you need to learn, absorb, and try, repeatedly.

CAVEAT: You don't need the "comic gene" to be funny, although I have to admit, there are people who are born funny. But these techniques and advice will not work if you have the unfunny gene. And we all know people like that. They just don't get it. They are marching to the beat of a different drummer and the drummer is Pete Best.

By the way, I used Pete Best to make a point—outdated references fail in the world of humor. Always use a fresh topical reference. However, since my list of drummers who are total losers begins and ends with Pete Best, we're stuck with him...although one more stint in rehab for Ringo and he could once again replace Pete. But I digress. There are people who are just genetically unfunny, who can't deliver a joke because they don't know what a joke is. A classic example—Russian president Vladimir Putin. Or Joe Piscopo.

So if you are a comedically-genetically-deformed person, return this book and get your money back.

However, if you are not in this infinitesimally small group, read on....

10 REASONS WHY
BEING FUNNY IS IMPORTANT

1. *Funny people have more friends.*

There are three ways in life to become popular: be rich, be beautiful, or be funny. Everyone likes being around witty, entertaining people who can make them laugh. It's why you rarely see pictures of Osama bin Laden sitting at the head table of a bar mitzvah.

2. *Funny people get noticed at work.*

No, we're not talking about the idiot who photocopies his buttocks in the mailroom, or the moron who wastes valuable Internet time forwarding non-original e-mails to everyone all day. We're talking about the employee who can keep people's interest during a presentation by being funny, the supervisor who can build loyalty and a sense of camaraderie through the bonding that comes with the sharing of a joke, or the security guard who can get a chuckle out of the angry, disgruntled employee.

3. *Funny people make more money.*

It's a proven fact that people who can make others laugh make more money. It's the reason the president only makes $400,000 a year, while Carrot Top pulls down $17 million.

4. *Funny people don't get wedgies in high school.*

Sheer physical bulk can prevent the humiliation of being given a wedgie by a gang of cretins. So can a sense of humor. A quick wit and the ability to get the leader of the cretins or the "Head Heather" to laugh can turn a tense high school confrontation into a fun-filled bonding situation. Or, you can just give them your lunch money and run.

5. *Funny people get better service in stores.*

Face it, the life of a sales clerk is not easy. It ranks somewhere between proctology assistant and Jennifer Lopez's wedding planner. So who are these vessels of failed dreams going to be more responsive to:

an angry trailer-park mom in curlers beating her kids upside the head in aisle 7 of K-mart while demanding to know where to find the size 44 polyester stretch pants, or you, someone who can make them laugh?

6. *Funny people live longer.*

George Burns, funny, lived to be one hundred. Milton Berle, funny, lived to be ninety-three. James Dean, not funny, dead at age twenty-four. I rest my case.

7. *Funny people are smarter.*

Maybe it's a direct link. Maybe to be funny, you need to be smart. You certainly need to be well read, able to connect seemingly unconnected events and pull topical references out and use them at the drop of a hat. And even if funny people aren't really smarter, they still seem that way. I really don't know if Bill Maher is smarter than President Bush but I do know this—Maher is funnier and certainly seems to have a better grasp of the economy.

8. *Being funny can cover up a multitude of sins.*

People might have been willing to overlook some of Saddam Hussein's human rights violations if he were killing at the Baghdad Chuckle House on open mike night. I know I would be a lot more forgiving.

9. *Funny people have more sex.*

   I mentioned this above as a key reason to buy this book. In the end, we all know it's true. If you can get someone to lower her barrier against laughter, you are more likely to get her to take off her clothes.

10. *Being funny is obviously important enough to you that you bought this book. So with that in mind, let us begin.*

HISTORY OF EARLY COMEDY

Here's a quick sketch of comedy up until the beginning of the modern era.

3500 B.C.: A twenty-three-year-old cave dweller in the south of France accidentally spears a neighbor in the buttocks while hunting antelope. Hilarious laughter ensues as comedy has its first victim. Moral: weird use of everyday items is funny.

Fifth century B.C.: Aristophanes writes a series of comedic plays in ancient Greece, gets to perform them in the amphitheater, kills with his opening joke of "Two members of the Hebrew tribe walk into a bar. They buy it."

1387: Geoffrey Chaucer invents the medieval comedy *Canterbury Tales,* which consists primarily of dirty jokes, double entendres, and people laughing at how he spells "Geoffrey."

Late 1500s: Shakespeare uses subtle wit and wordplay in his early works. Since 98 percent of commoners can't read, this goes nowhere and he goes back to his bread and butter—insult humor:

"You blocks, you stones, you worse than senseless things." *Julius Caesar,* Act I, Scene i.

"This sanguine coward, this bed presser, this horseback breaker, this huge hill of flesh." *Henry IV Part One,* Act II, Scene iv.

1600–1923: No comedy; people are too preoccupied with the pox, plague, and overthrowing colonial tyrants.

1924: The Marx Brothers.

2.

The Building Blocks
of Being Funny

THE 13 RULES (A Joker's Dozen)

1. Be Smart, Be Topical

The number-one rule at the top of the comedy pyramid, the one thing you need to get from your investment in this book, is to be smart and topical. Because if you are smart and topical and *always prepared to react with that smart, topical observation,* you will be funnier than you are right now.

To do this, you have to know what is out there that is funny. Read a newspaper, watch *Headline News,* buy a tabloid, read *People* magazine. You need to know what people are talking about, thinking about, and what's "in" in the pop culture. When it's summer, hot jokes are in; when we're fighting terrorists, camel sodomy jokes are in. You need to read the newspaper, watch the news, and be informed so that in any situation, you are ready to key in on a word and deliver a killer line.

You need to work on it every day. You need to associate seemingly different unrelated topics (hence the word *topical*) and connect the dots in your mind so that funny words and phrases come rolling off your tongue like sweat off of Martha Stewart's stockbroker.

Here's an example of being current and topical. Let's say you are ready to deliver a line about someone's intelligence—remember, even though he may have set the all-time standard for public dumb, Dan Quayle has been unemployed and out of the news since 1992. Keanu Reeves, Mr. Matrix himself, is still working, still making movies, and he is still dumb.

There's a time lag in the publication of any book but here are some good current event references from January 2003:

DRUNK: in, Ozzy Osbourne, Diana Ross; out, Jan-Michael Vincent

QUEEN BITCH: in, Martha Stewart; out, Kathie Lee

NUTS: in, Michael Jackson, once again; out, Farrah Fawcett and Anne Heche

SLUT: in, Christina Aguilera; out, Madonna

GAY: in, Liza's husband, one of the New York Mets; out, Siegfried and Roy

FAT: in, Anna Nicole Smith; out, Liz Taylor and Marlon Brando

MALE SLUT: Look, I know he's an old reference but Bill Clinton is the Michael Jordan, John Elway, Wayne Gretzky, and Babe Ruth of hounds.

TOPICAL CELEBRITY REFERENCES: CAREER VERSUS PEAK VALUE

One of the smartest, funniest men I have ever read is baseball statistician Bill James. One of the tools he uses in explaining his evaluation of players is the concept of peak value versus career value. A classic example for pitchers would be Sandy Koufax compared with Don Sutton. Koufax had a huge peak value for a few years but his career was relatively short; Sutton at his best was nowhere near the pitcher Koufax was, yet for over twenty years, year in and year out, Sutton had real value.

The same is true of comedy references. These are the people you can use in your jokes or people you can make fun of in conversation. The peak-value references are those who, during their prime, dominated the news and office lunch conversations. Those with great career value became human commas, shorthand for the problems and mistakes we all make in our pathetic little lives, mistakes that they made on the big stage.

Some, like John Wayne Bobbitt, have a high peak value for a few weeks or months; others, like Ted Kennedy, are consistent for laughs year in and year out.

Here are the top references of my comedy lifetime.

Peak Value

10. John Wayne Bobbitt: peak years 1993–94. There are those who would argue his porn movie career in the late 1990s should count toward his peak value. I figure, if Fox doesn't think he's good enough for *Celebrity Boxing,* then he's not good enough to move up on this list.

9. Joey Buttafuoco: peak years 1993–95, 2002. His name alone earns him a spot on this list. *Celebrity Boxing* brought him back briefly last year.

8. Bob Dole: peak years 1994–96, 1999–2001. I knew Bob Dole as a war hero and a good senator. My daughter thinks he's just some old guy who took Viagra and made a Pepsi commercial with Britney Spears.

7. Heidi Fleiss: peak years 1993–95. She could have moved up on the list if she had named names. Nice Jewish girl. Not married. I guess she just hasn't found the right NBA team.

6. Charlie Sheen: peak years 1991–2002. Charlie's chance to become an all-time career hall-of-famer was cut tragically short by a happy marriage.

5. Frank Gifford: peak years 1996–98. When you think of Frank, do you think of his hall-of-fame football career? Do you think of a legendary *Monday Night Football* broadcaster? Nah, you think of Frank balls deep in a middle-aged flight attendant.

4. Paula Jones: peak years 1992–98. She beats Frank Gifford by a nose.

3. Monica Lewinsky: peak years 1997–2003. How many people's names have become synonymous with a sex act? She's Heidi Fleiss without the brains and naked ambition; she's Anna Nicole Smith without the acting ability and TV show. But most of all, she's a woman who kept a dress with a stain on it.

2. Tonya Harding: peak years 1994–2002. What's great about Tonya is she keeps reinventing herself. She's gone from white trash figure skater to white trash honeymoon video girl to white trash drunk to white trash Celebrity Boxer. It's a long shot but with just a few more arrests, she could make it up there on the all-time career list.

TIED WITH

Mike Tyson: 1990–2002. I don't count the years when Mike was actually winning fights. I consider

Mike's peak years when he lost huge fights to Buster Douglas and to Robin Givens. Plus, he bit a man's ear in a heavyweight championship fight. Enough said.

1. Anna Nicole Smith: peak years 1994–2003. She's white trash, she's got giant breasts, she has an IQ of sixty, she's got her own TV show, she's a gold digger, and she married a ninety-year-old.

There are a few worthy people who just missed the cut, like Pamela Anderson, Pee-wee Herman, Boy George, Anne Heche, Daryl Strawberry, and Robert Downey Jr. Each of them could do something in the next few years to reestablish their peak value but at this point, they are more likely to end up on *Celebrity Mole* than in this list of legends.

Career Value

10. Hugh Hefner: 1954–present. Pretty one-dimensional but when you think of out-of-control hormones and juvenile, teenage lust, you think of Hef. Plus, he's seventy-seven and still dating twins.

9. Keith Richards: 1964–present. Drug users like Robert Downey Jr., Steve Howe, Marion Barry, and Daryl Strawberry didn't make it on the list because

they became sad and pathetic. They took all the fun out of recreational drug use. Let's be honest—Keith Richards is the kind of substance abuser who always brings a smile to your face.

8. Martha Stewart: 1990–present. Thirty seconds on her cell and she went from the peak-value list to the career-value list; from the woman all men and a few women love to hate to a woman the SEC loves to hate.

7. Madonna: 1984–present. Her relatively peaceful marriage to the father of baby number two has marked the end of her tramp era. Name another celebrity who has had sex with people ranging from Warren Beatty in a hotel suite to a busboy in the backseat of a Chevy. At one point J. Lo showed promise but she's too high-class. Sadly, there are no great tramps out there to take Madonna's place, although with one more video like "Dirty," Christina Aguilera could make a run at the title. And just when Madonna was in danger of being relegated to the peak-value list as a reformed slut, her experimentation with mystic Jewish religions and incredibly bad acting ensured that she ended up one of the all-time greats.

6. Hillary Clinton: 1991–present. We've gone from Madonna the tramp to Hillary the anti-tramp. It's

still too early to tell whether she could move up on the chart. Maybe it's a vast right-wing conspiracy that's keeping her off. Keep your fingers crossed that she runs for president.

5. The royal family: A.D. 1215–present. For almost eight hundred years, these people have indulged in incest in the guise of love, inbred, sponged off the taxpayers, sucked their financial adviser's toes in public, committed adultery, and ruined a once great empire. You've got to love them just for their longevity. I bet Copernicus was telling jokes about them.

4. Ted Kennedy: 1962–present. If the Corleones are America's most famous powerful fictional family, the Kennedys are the most powerful real family...and Teddy is the Fredo. The only difference is when Teddy went into the lake, he came out alive. He's larger than life. In fact, he's larger than Monaco.

3. Kathie Lee Gifford: 1980s–present. From her early days as a Hee Haw Honey to her reinvention as a TV star to her perfect marriage to her soap opera with Frank to her running that sweatshop, she has been the woman even Martha Stewart fans love to hate.

2. Michael Jackson: 1970–present. We've watched Michael grow from an extremely talented young

African-American male from a dysfunctional family to a middle-aged white woman who lives with a chimp, llama, and giraffe and who likes young boys. Let me mention some other weirdness—the bones of the elephant man, the Klingon general's uniform, the glove, the surgical mask, the nose falling off, and dangling the baby. And that was just on one weekend.

1. Bill Clinton: 1988–present. What else needs to be said?

2. *Use Funny Words and Sounds*

Woody Allen once wrote a great piece that consisted solely of funny words. They're words that just sound funny the minute you read them. The standard rule of comedy is that *k* words are funny (and who hasn't laughed at the word *kike*?), but there are plenty of other words that work. Try them out and see. These are all good words to use: tramp, shtupping, imbecile, pants, breeder's hips, chicken, loin, melons, hooters, kinky, slut, bimbo, male whore, buffoon.

Whenever I work with Billy Crystal, we always try, if at all possible, to work the word *sheetcake* into his routine. You don't just make an offer he can't refuse to Marlon Brando, you make him an offer of brisket and a sheetcake.

I once told a joke about a Disney-style theme park opening in Iran that ended with the comparison of Mickey Mouse to their mascot, "Hezbollah Mouse." I don't know why, but if you say the words *Hezbollah Mouse* out loud, it makes people laugh.

> **"Painting a vivid visual picture with words is funny.**
> *It was a very obvious toupee. It had a zipper."*
> **—Rita Rudner**

And in choosing words, always remember that specific is better than general. The specific product *Durashears* is a better word to use than the generic item *scissors*. Saying you went to Hooters is always funnier than just saying you went to a strip club.

Gilbert Gottfried was asked a question on *Hollywood Squares*: "What is the best thing to do for a hairy back?" Gilbert's answer: "I close my eyes and pretend she's wearing an alpaca sweater." What made the joke work? The word *alpaca*.

In addition you can always use sound effects. That's right, you're your own foley artist. Whenever comic Eddie Driscoll talks about sex, he pretends to open up his pants with a zip-flop sound effect.

3. *Understand the Hidden Truth*

Anything you say that is funny will, to some degree, have a hidden truth behind it. Jerry Seinfeld recently told *Time* magazine that "every great joke uncovers something." One of the reasons I wanted to write for Jay Leno was that the first time I saw his act, with every story and joke he told, I immediately identified with it and with his point of view. I saw the hidden truths, the common "What's stupid about this?" that I (we) can all recognize.

> "Every comedian knows that the embarrassing incident they had and the thoughts they had afterward are shared by 80 percent of the people in the audience because our DNA is so similar. Funny people say out loud what the rest of the world is thinking."
>
> —Andy Breckman

For fun, once a week on KTRS in St. Louis, I do a ten-minute segment of "What is pissing Jon off this week." It's my hobby, a non-standup version of Jay's "What's my beef" or of Dennis Miller's rants. I take really stupid stories in the news and point out the ridiculousness of the truth.

I did this one bit last summer when I heard on the radio that a California health official was suggesting the way to prevent West Nile virus was to bring more mosquito-eating bats into the state. I made the point that only a public official would think a good solution to West Nile is the spread of rabies. Not only that, this is the worst possible combination for California—Ozzy Osbourne and two million bats!

4. Have a Target

And now for the one thing about being funny that civilians are in denial about—all humor has to have a target. Comedy isn't pretty—the reason comedians say they kill is because there is a victim. The victim can be you, it can be someone not present in the room, it can be a common close enemy or a distant, foreign enemy. It can be a small target like a waiter who annoyed you or a big target like the government or terrorists. But in the end if you want something funny to hit its mark, you need a target to aim at. So in any situation, in any conversation, know who you want to make fun of and make sure he or she is a worthy target. As you're practicing, as you're out there flexing your funny muscles, there are easy targets you can always nail. Sure, they're layups. But layups still count as two points.

Easy Targets

States: West Virginia, Arkansas, New Jersey, Florida, or the state bordering your home state on the south or west

Safe stereotypes: Blondes, lawyers, ex-lovers

Celebrities: (see peak- and career-value list, above)

Cities: New York, L.A., Kabul, Detroit

Sports teams: Cubs, Bengals, Red Sox

People with boring jobs: accountants, government employees

> **"People in positions of power making stupid mistakes is funny—i.e., George Bush and his problem with multisyllabled words."**
>
> **—Rita Rudner**

....

> **"The butt of the joke should always be fictional, yourself, or someone powerful."**
>
> **—James Carville**

5. *Have a Point of View*

This is really a corollary of the last two rules—you need to take a chance to be funny. You need to be willing to expose the bitter truth about a situation or person, target that victim, and deliver your take on it. You need to be willing to "risk the crickets" for the reward of getting the laugh. "Crickets" is what we call it at *The Tonight Show* when someone tells a joke and there's dead silence in the room and all you can hear are crickets chirping.

I don't know how many times that the politicians and corporate leaders I write for say, "Give me only jokes that work." Well, I don't know what will work; God doesn't know that. I give them the best jokes I can come up with and cross my fingers that they work. Plus I make sure to get paid in advance.

Jay Leno reads and writes some fifteen hundred jokes a day to get twenty for that night's monologue, and on any given night, there are one or two that might not get a laugh. He's the best there is and if he occasionally gets crickets, so will you.

It's okay, you'll live. Just understand that no one bats a thousand.

6. Surprise Them

"Surprise in any form is always funny—overstatement, understatement, cruelty, comparatives."
—Rita Rudner

One key element to being funny is surprise. There are at least five ways you can surprise people with humor. The first three are self-evident. The two that I think work the best I'll explain in more detail.

1. *You can say something funny in the middle of a serious conversation or situation.*

2. *You can say something funny in response to a person who is expecting a serious answer to a question.*

3. *You can say something funny in a location no one expects humor (like a funeral home or an elevator).*

4. *You can say something outrageous with a deadpan delivery.*

"Don't be afraid. Once you get used to doing it, it's like throwing a switch, so you can go from being very serious to suddenly dropping in a joke and then back to being serious. My audiences get confused and usually can't tell which is which. But that's another problem to discuss another time."

—Garry Shandling

Garry is one of the best at using a deadpan delivery. In any conversation with him, he can go from being serious to delivering a great joke and then immediately back. That's his real personality and his onstage persona; for you, being deadpan is not your comic persona, but rather a way to get a laugh by using a surprise technique in your delivery.

23

I find a deadpan delivery works great in response to someone sharing a completely useless fact or after someone has uttered some stupid cliché or phrase. For example, if someone says, "It was raining at our company picnic, can you imagine anything worse?" answer with something like "How about being sexually assaulted by an aroused goat? That would be worse."

A few months ago I was walking down the hall at NBC Burbank when a newswoman dropped something, said, "Oh, shit," and then, seeing me, said, "Pardon my French." My response was to say in a very informative, know-it-all voice, "Actually in French it's *le gran crape*."

5. *You can say the opposite of what's expected.*

EXAMPLE: Whenever someone has to change an appointment, and this happens all the time in L.A.—for example, when the hairdresser bumps you for a more important client—I'll always say something the next time I go in. Something like "Sorry about the change in time, I hope I didn't cause any problems when I had to rearrange things to accommodate your schedule because after all, you're paying me. Wait a second, I'm sorry, I have that backwards, I pay you. My bad."

ANOTHER EXAMPLE: Eighty-four-year-old Hall of Fame baseball broadcaster Ernie Harwell was being interviewed for a news story on his retirement at Comerica Park in Detroit last summer. A number of fans were watching him being interviewed. He turned to them and said, "These camerapeople are from HBO. We're doing a segment for *Sex and the City*."

7. *The Key to Comedy . . . Timing*

For the professional comic, the timing within the structure of the joke is of critical importance. For the civilian, there are two different elements of comedic timing. The first involves *putting the funny at the end*.

You remember the rule "Never end a sentence with a preposition"?; also remember to always put the funny words at the end. Whatever you do, do not drag out and dilute the punch of your punch line . . . by adding words . . . at the end . . . that drag out . . . the point . . . you are trying to make. Get it? Really, do you?

RIGHT WAY: VH1 planned a TV show about Liza Minnelli and her husband. It's called *Queer As Folk*.

WRONG WAY: There's a new TV show being planned about Liza Minnelli and her husband. *Queer As Folk* is the name of it and it's on cable television.

For the other type of timing, let's go to an expert for his take. Jeffrey Ross is considered the top roast and insult comic in America. You've seen him on the Comedy Central roasts of Hugh Hefner and Drew Carey. He performs at all the top comedy clubs in the country and has been on *The Tonight Show, Conan,* and *Hollywood Squares.*

> **"The truth is, when you're sitting around with friends and you think of a funny line, don't blurt it out. Hold a funny line to the right moment. You want to be patient so you can get a good clear shot, when people aren't talking and the focus is on you and your line. It can turn a B line into an A."**
>
> **—Jeffrey Ross**

8. *Tag the Joke and Do a Run*

A tag to a joke in *The Tonight Show* monologue occurs when Jay gives the setup, the twist, and the joke and then adds an afterthought, a second punch line. A run is an entire series of similar jokes on the same subject.

JAY'S EXAMPLE OF A TAG

JOKE: Did you see Anna Nicole Smith's new show on the E! channel? I think *E* stands for "enormous."
TAG: Forget E!, it should be on the Food Channel.

A tag for a civilian can also mean a quick response to finish someone else's thought. Your job as a funny person is to decide if the situation is ripe for a joke, take the serious statement someone has made, and tag it. It usually works when someone has uttered a cliché and tried to pass it off as wisdom.

CLICHÉ: He'd give you the shirt off his back.
TAG: What would I want with a sweaty size-48 shirt?

CLICHÉ: At least he's not suffering anymore.
TAG: What if he's burning in hell?

CLICHÉ: My mom used to say, feed a fever, starve a cold.
TAG: And Valtrex for everything else.

A run is when you think of a joke and then keep coming up with a series of tags.

EXAMPLE: Someone asks you if you have ever seen an adult movie. Your answer—"Sure, I've seen all the classics. *Forrest Hump; Schindler's Lust; Dude, Where's My Vibrator; Sweet Ho Alabama; Star Whores; Mr. Holland's Anus...*"

EXAMPLE: This is a run of some of the Hannibal Lecter jokes Jay did when the movie *Red Dragon* came out:

What does Hannibal call a supermodel from Wisconsin—a quarter-pounder with cheese.

What does Hannibal call a van full of senior citizens—meals on wheels.

What does Hannibal call Strom Thurmond—a stale cracker.

What does Hannibal call the singer Meatloaf—meat loaf.

EXAMPLE: At the taping of the *ABC Fiftieth Anniversary Special,* I was backstage in a very crowded area when a production assistant suggested I stand on the giant C used in the ABC prop they had been using on stage. The C was wobbly and when she said "Come stand by the C" I went into a play-on-words run:

I can't, I get C-sick.

Most women don't want a C-section.

Get Gavin McLeod over here and we have the old man
and the C.
This is my first C since math class.

Not a great run but a quick run that worked because it
was just so stupid.

9. *Keep It Short*

Leave it to Bill Cosby to tell a funny fifteen-minute story.
Your goal is to deliver a short, punchy remark—thus the
term punch line.

Perhaps the best example of this is on *Hollywood
Squares*. I've written for the show for the past five years
and what works is when Tom Bergeron asks a star a question and he or she delivers a short one-liner. You can
always tell the stars who aren't comics—they add unnec-
essary words to the joke, stretch it out, and don't realize
that people have disconnected in that fifteen seconds
from the setup (the question). At that point, seeing that
they're losing the audience, they commit the cardinal sin
of bailing on the joke, not getting the laugh, and making
its failure a self-fulfilling prophecy. (Actually, most cardinal sins nowadays involve a cardinal and Cub Scout
pack 257, but that's for my next book.)

Note the exception is a comic who can really perform
the lines—a Brad Garrett, Ellen DeGeneres, a Gilbert
Gottfried, Arsenio, or a Martin Mull. They don't need to

give a short, quick joke because they are masters at playing the audience. For civilians, stick to the short, tried and true.

Let's take a look at some classic *Hollywood Squares* questions and their jokes. These are from shows that ran in September 2002.

QUESTION TO JOAN RIVERS: True or false? Ladies who would like to return to their youth can pay a doctor $3,500 for an operation to be revirginized.
JOAN'S JOKE: Save money. Turn off the light and leave on your panty hose.

QUESTION TO TRIUMPH THE INSULT COMIC DOG: Who is the only dog to ever make *People* magazine's best-dressed list?
TRIUMPH'S JOKE: Sally Jessy Raphaël.

QUESTION TO NICOLE SULLIVAN: What popularized the saying "Strong enough for a man but made for a woman"?
NICOLE'S JOKE: k.d. lang.

10. Hit a Triple

Baseball players hit home runs. Funny people want to hit triples because things are funnier in threes. Think of the first jokes you ever heard—there's a reason so many jokes begin with "a priest, a minister, and a rabbi."

Triples for a civilian work best when prepared and delivered in a speech.

> "Today we gather to honor the person who has made this company what it is today [1]: someone who is the driving force behind our success [2], someone who has the brilliant ideas and vision our company is known for [3]. But Jack's wife could not be here today...so instead we honor Jack."

But a triple can also work in a run or in a story. All you need to do in your preparation is think of three points.

TWO TRIPLES I LOVE: The first is from *The Tonight Show*.

> "Today is the anniversary of the Watergate break-in. When you think about it, Richard Nixon and Bill Clinton had a lot in common. They both had ethics problems, both faced impeachment, and both were nicknamed Tricky Dick."

Another triple is from Billy Crystal's roast of Rob Reiner.

> "Rob is now Mr. Inside Politics. Rob calls the president Bill. He calls the vice president Al. And he calls Domino's five times a week."

Last year at the Emmys, on a taped piece in the middle of a very serious tribute to Oprah as she was receiving the first-ever Bob Hope Humanitarian Award, right in between all these big, serious speakers like Coretta Scott King, Julia Roberts, and Tom Cruise, Chris Rock went the other way and combined two things—surprise (by using humor where no one expected it) and a triple (actually he hit a triple and then brought it home with a tag).

"I watch Oprah. I read *Oprah* magazine. I use Oprah toothpaste. I even use Oprah hair care products."

—Chris Rock

11. Sell the Joke

This is the corollary to keeping it short. SELL THE JOKE. Know that you are funny, know that what you say is funny, and don't bail at the end...

12. Take It to the Next Step/The What-If...

You can be funny by giving a simple reaction to what someone else is saying. But you can be really really funny if you take it to the next step. This is what I call the "what-if." My favorite current what-if on television is the show *Monk,* written by my friend Andy Breckman, whom I've worked with twice on the Oscars when Steve

Martin was host. Andy's what-if involved this: What if the smartest and best detective in San Francisco was obsessive-compulsive? The result? One of the best shows on television.

Don't think on just one level, take it to another dimension. If someone is talking about UN efforts to modernize and rebuild Afghanistan, the quick, easy response is to say they're shipping over thousands of tons of brand-new rocks. The what-if is to ask, "What if we help them build modern strip malls? Can you imagine a strip mall in Kandahar? What's the Blockbuster like over there? The number-one movie is *Dude, Where's My Camel.*"

> EXAMPLE: There was a story in the news of how England is suffering a huge shortage of sperm donors and as a result, we are shipping over sperm. My what-if added the factor of "What if we were helping them the same way we were helping feed the people of Somalia and Afghanistan? Can you imagine if it was like those food drops? We're airdropping sperm. And you thought people in Kabul hated being hit in the head with some frozen corn."

13. Always Ask, What's Stupid About This?

I put this at the end of the chapter that began with the Golden Rule of "Be smart, be topical" so that you begin with the most important rule and you end with the one surefire question to ask yourself to help get you thinking funny.

It's the best comedy question of all time, it gives you a target, it enables you to take things to the next level or to the absurd conclusion. Take a look at a situation and ask, What's stupid about this?

EXAMPLE: Last October I flew back to Philadelphia to see my parents. As I was driving through my hometown and getting acclimated to it again, I saw a project with the names of members of the Philadelphia Anti-Graffiti Taskforce—*spray-painted on the wall of a building.* You see that and you have to ask—What's stupid about this?

TYPES OF HUMOR

Self-Deprecation

"I would never want to belong to a country club that would have me as a member."

—Groucho Marx

. . . .

"I remember the first time I realized I could make people laugh. It was in the third year of my show."

—Conan O'Brien

Self-deprecating humor may be the single most important technique a public speaker can use. It's an instant way to establish a rapport with an audience, a way for someone powerful—and if you're holding the microphone, you are automatically perceived as powerful—to let everyone know that you don't take yourself too seriously. Even if the topic is serious, it's a great way to signal that you understand that underneath our clothes, we're all naked and one day, we all end up dead. Or in the case of Ted Williams, frozen.

Self-deprecation is also a useful comedy tool for the everyday person making everyday conversation because the ability to make fun of yourself is a way to open up to someone and let him or her into your space and world in a way that you control. In a strange way, it also shows great confidence, that you are comfortable with who you are and strong enough to not take yourself too seriously.

To some, Carrie Fisher is Princess Leia; to those who know her and her work since *Star Wars,* she is an incredibly gifted wordsmith, one of the highest-paid "script doctors" in the world, and one of the funniest people I have ever talked to or exchanged e-mails with.

> **"One way to be funny is to talk in public about yourself like you're talking behind your own back. Self-deprecation has the great advantage of looking like self-awareness covered with the charm of humility. Whenever you can talk about the absurdity of yourself as a human being, it's funny."**
> **—Carrie Fisher**

Bob Ellison, whose credits include writing for the Emmys, the *Mary Tyler Moore Show,* and *Rhoda,* says that to him, the key is this: *Rather than put someone else down, put yourself down; it makes you more human and it gets people on your side.*

EXAMPLES OF CELEBRITIES WHO USE SELF-DEPRECATING HUMOR

Terry Bradshaw is a great motivational speaker who begins his remarks by making fun of his hair, his marriages, his mom, and his intelligence. It's a great way for Terry to establish a rapport with the audience and to play off some of the things he's known for. The truth is, if Terry were really that dumb, how did he end up being the only NFL quarterback to win four Super Bowl rings? Rather than brag about himself, Terry starts every speech with a few jokes. It connects him to people in the room and it shows he can laugh at himself; and, if you can laugh at yourself, people can laugh with you.

Every celebrity who is a good public speaker knows how to win over the audience with self-deprecating humor: Arnold Schwarzenegger begins his speeches with jokes about his accent, his acting ability, and his marriage to a Kennedy; Roseanne and Tom Arnold used to introduce themselves as everyone's worst nightmare, white trash with money.

One of the more remarkable examples of effectively using self-deprecating humor came from a time I saw the not-yet-famous James Carville giving a speech.

Before James became the legend he is today, his track record in campaigns was probably about three wins and fifteen losses, but everyone could tell he had the charisma and intelligence to become a star. One day I watched him speak at a convention of political consultants. For three hours, consultant after consultant got up and bragged about how many winning campaigns they had run, how smart they were, how unblemished their records. Then came Carville. He started his speech by saying what an honor it was to have been invited to be with such great consultants. He said he figured the reason they invited him was because he was the one they had been beating all those years. This one remark did two things—it made James the only likeable person in a group of pompous asses, and second, it immediately threw some doubt on the credibility of what had been said before.

Imagine how much more sympathetic a character Martha Stewart would be right now if for once in her life she had admitted that the three-story house she built from rubber bands, mulch, and two-day-old bread didn't turn out quite the way she expected. It would make her fleecing of ImClone all the more bearable.

My Experience

I used self-deprecation in the first speech I ever gave, to an audience of lawyers, all of whom were Ivy League types. I opened by telling them I had graduated from Villanova Law School, which has a lot in common with Harvard. Specifically, the letters *V* and *A*.

TIPS

- Make yourself part of the group that you are addressing but set yourself apart by divulging a setback or disaster that happened to you.
- Make fun of the obvious about yourself if you are well known by your audience.

- If you're rich and people know it, admit it. President John F. Kennedy once told an audience that his father offered to buy him a win in the West Virginia primary, not a landslide. Joan Rivers handled her obvious new face-lift by telling the audience that her grandkids call her "Nanny New Face."
- If you are not known by your audience, tell them a fact about yourself so you can make fun of it.
- Surprise them by setting them off in one direction, where they think you're going to inflate your own balloon, and then deflate it yourself. Arnold Schwarzenegger tells a great joke about how he has lived the American dream, that he is proof that any immigrant can come here and become rich simply by perseverance, working hard, and marrying a Kennedy.

WARNING: Self-deprecation does not mean self-flagellation. Spending fifteen minutes berating yourself doesn't say that you're funny, it says you are a loser. A classic example is Al Gore making fun of himself for being stiff. One or two jokes are funny. Ten jokes are too much— and, repeated over and over, they only served to remind people that he really is a stiff.

THE POINT TO REMEMBER
In a crowd of blowhards and braggarts, the ability to take a funny shot at yourself sets you above the crowd.

YOUR HOMEWORK ASSIGNMENT

1. *Think of something you are well known for.*

2. *Make up two jokes about yourself that reference that fact.*

Exaggeration

"One billion people around the world are watching the Oscar telecast tonight and they're all thinking the same thing—we're all gay."

—Steve Martin

"American Taliban fighter John Walker Lindh is supposedly gay. Do you know what that means—the Taliban is more tolerant than the Boy Scouts."

—Jay Leno

Let's say you're out with friends and talking about an idiot coworker. Saying he has an IQ of 105 doesn't make the point. Moderation isn't funny. Overexaggeration is funny, for it enables you to make a serious point in a memorable way. If two women are talking and one says she bought her husband a Sharper Image Turbo Groomer for his nose hair, that's a fact. If she had to buy him a weed whacker—now that's funny.

EXAMPLES: When James Carville gives a speech, he always makes fun of LSU. It actually took James a few extra semesters to get through there, but saying it took him five years to gradu- ate doesn't make his point. That's why he always tells the audience he set a scholastic record at LSU. He got fifty-four hours of F"s.

When Paul Reiser was the emcee at the 2002 City of Hope Spirit Awards, he spoke to an audience of record company executives who were there to honor the six presidents of the movie studio music divisions. Here is his run, which ended in exaggeration. As an exercise, see if you can count how many different types of jokes he uses.

"The six people we are honoring tonight sold something like 185 million sound tracks this year. There are approximately five billion people in the world. Let's do the math because not all of them buy sound tracks. My mother has never bought a sound track of anything. I have never bought one and neither have any of my friends so now we're down eleven. No one in China has ever bought any because they make bootleg copies of everything. No one over forty-nine really buys sound tracks and no one under twenty-five has bought them because they're busy downloading them for free. So that means this year, each of you in this room has bought 47,000 units.

What makes this so funny? Here's the analysis:
- "so now we're down eleven" (self-deprecation).
- "they make bootleg copies of everything" (hidden truth).
- "busy downloading them for free" (hidden truth).
- "each of you in this room bought 47,000 units" (exaggeration).

In that one sequence ending with an exaggeration, Paul Reiser used three different types of jokes.

My Experience

I had a girlfriend who was kind of easy. When I described her post-breakup, I let everyone know we had a problem because she slept with her boss. And she worked for the Vatican. She used to date the Oakland Raiders but only because there are only fifteen players on a hockey team. She bought her condoms at the Price Club—in bulk.

TIPS

- Exaggeration can work in any and every funny situation.
- It works not only as the punch line, but in making each part of a story stand out.

WARNING: At some point in using this to be funny, you will overexaggerate so that the person focuses too much on your example and misses the humor. If James Carville said he had six thousand hours of F's at LSU, you'd spend too much time trying to figure out how many years that is. Fifty-four hours of F's makes the point.

THE POINT TO REMEMBER
Exaggeration involves taking something true and embellishing it to make it funny

YOUR HOMEWORK ASSIGNMENT

1. *Take a failure or setback from your day, e.g., traffic on the way home from work.*

2. *Tell it to a friend with exaggeration.*

Sarcasm

> "The Center for Disease Control has announced some tips for avoiding West Nile virus. They're telling people not to pick up any dead crows. There goes my weekend plans."
>
> —Jay Leno

Skip this chapter. Anyone who went to a state school like you did is not going to get it.

Okay, just read slowly.

That, my friends, is an example of sarcasm.

Sarcasm is both an attitude and a willingness to use a joke and make a point. It's the stating of a truth in such a way that it counts as social commentary. To be funny and sarcastic, you always need to be on the alert for that moment when a government official, a salesperson you deal with, a coworker or estranged family member, says something stupid that needs to be ridiculed. It is your tool to make a social comment and be funny.

EXAMPLES: Jay did a great joke when L.A. officials announced they were opening up "baby dropoff centers," which are places where, for seventy-two hours, women can drop off their babies if they don't want them, no questions asked. Jay's joke: "That's what I love about California. You get seventy-two hours to return your baby if you don't want it, but if you buy a car you don't like, you're stuck with it."

SITUATION: The CEO of your company, who makes $2 million a year, lays off five hundred workers but takes a $5 million end-of-the-year bonus.
SARCASTIC LINE: "I support him. It's tough to try and scrape by on two million dollars a year."

SITUATION: Jeb Bush's daughter gets arrested for illegal prescription drugs.
SARCASTIC LINE: "At least someone in the Bush family has a prescription drug plan."

My Experience

My local school district suspended two students for having sex at school by sending them home for the day. My reaction—There's a good idea; punish a juvenile delinquent and a nymphomaniac by sending them to a deserted house with no supervision for an afternoon.

TIPS

- Pick a big target.
- Use a stock "transitional phrase," like "There's a good idea," to help you buy time as the mental file cards flip and you signal to the listener that you are about to use sarcasm.

- Use sarcasm to make a point when the mood is angry, not when you're having a good time.

WARNING: Sarcasm during good times can come off as sour grapes. Commenting about President Bush's lack of understanding about the economy won't really connect with your audience if the Dow is at 12,000. It works much better if you critique his tax cut for the rich when the Dow is at 8,000. Then the joke works when you point out that a tax cut for the rich only benefits the Bush family.

THE POINT TO REMEMBER

Sarcasm is saying something that means the exact opposite of what you're saying.

YOUR HOMEWORK ASSIGNMENT

1. *Watch the news.*

2. *Find a government decision and look for the hidden truth about it.*

3. *Make your funny sarcastic comment.*

> **4.** *Or make a comment about this true story. At a Septem-*
> *ber 2002 environmental summit in South Africa, dele-*
> *gates generated over thirty tons of trash, waste*
> *containers were overflowing, and less than 20 percent*
> *of the trash was recycled.*

Outrageousness/Working Blue/Shock Value

"So Robert Blake claims he and his wife didn't
get along, he took her to dinner, he leaves for a
minute, and some stranger came up and shot
her. No man gets that lucky."

—Garry Shandling

In a day and age where priests are impregnating more
women than an NBA player, is there anything too outrageous to say? The limit of what you can say, as First
Amendment lawyers will point out, is dependent on
time, place, and manner. Just as you can't yell "fire" in a
crowded movie theater, you don't want to talk to
grandma about sodomy. Unless you have a really cool
grandma who has been known to pop the false teeth.

But first you need to understand why outrageous
shock humor works: it has the element essential to being
funny—the element of surprise.

EXAMPLES: *See* George Carlin. His "Seven Words You Can Never Say on Television" is a classic.

Chris Rock has a great routine about the Jerry Lewis telethon in which he talks about fifty years, hundreds of millions of dollars raised, and not one of those kids has ever walked. He says forget the research, use the money to get one of those kids a lap dance.

My Experience

During last year's giant Colorado and Arizona wildfires, I'd walk into a roomful of coworkers, look at the TV, and say, "Is it just me or does a wildfire sexually stimulate everyone?" Then I'd walk out of the room.

Or when people in my town would talk about the creepy-looking coach in our baseball league, I'd say his favorite pickup technique was to cruise by a preschool and ask a five-year-old if he wanted to help him find his lost puppy. He's the reason we have Amber Alerts.

WORKING BLUE
BEHIND THE SCENES AT THE OSCARS

During the Oscars last year the writers were sitting around the room eating, which is what writers do approximately fifteen hours a day, and I told Carrie Fisher that my thirteen-year-old daughter wanted to wear a thong. I was against it and my wife didn't know how to deal with it. The next day Carrie came in with a present for my daughter, what she said was a very tasteful thong appropriate for a thirteen-year-old. It was wrapped up and I thought, if Princess Leia says it's okay, it must be okay. So I brought it home and gave it to my daughter. When we opened it, it was a piece of pink string from an adult sex shop with a giant tongue on the front.

TIPS

- Know your audience.
- Don't rely on the *F* word. Instead, say something outrageous in a situation where no one expects it.
- If you're white, don't even attempt to say *motherfucker*. There's nothing more pathetic than Buffy from Connecticut trying to sound like she's Wanda Sykes. I suggest going the opposite way, like Conan O'Brien, and come off as really really white.

WARNING: Getting a great laugh is not worth the sexual harassment lawsuit. Be 100 percent sure of your audience.

THE POINT TO REMEMBER

There's always a fine line between outrageousness and really bad taste. If you work "blue," you will offend people. There will be casualties and one of the casualties may be you.

YOUR HOMEWORK ASSIGNMENT

1. *Go out with a same-gender peer group.*

2. *Pick what is perceived as a well-respected, innocent target.*

3. *Go wild, using your what-if and outrageousness to make fun of that person.*

Wordplay

"The transvestite wanted to eat, drink, and be Mary."

—George Carlin

....

"My mom lives in a gated community. Prison."

—Terry Bradshaw

"Yasir Arafat has been accused of stealing $1.3 billion from his organization. PLO? Sounds more like a CEO."

—Jay Leno

This really involves the technique of association. You're taking a word, twisting it, and using it to get a laugh. It works great as a response to a key word a friend has said to you in conversation; it also works extremely well for public speakers during Q & A.

EXAMPLES: We did a bit on *The Tonight Show* a while ago after a report that television programs were once again being broadcast on Kabul TV. We then listed some of the programs from the Afghanistan *TV Guide: Allah McBeal, Everybody Loves Ramadan, Camel and Greg.*

Or let's say Mom announces that your twenty-five-year-old cousin is dating a seventy-five-year-old man. Here's how it works. You instantly take the word *old* and flip through the file cards in your head looking for all the words associated with old: antique, May-December, ancient, dusty. So your response to your mom's announcement is you heard they met watching her favorite TV program, *Antiques Roadshow*. It's a May-December relationship. He may live until December.

51

My Experience

I was giving a speech to a Mensa group in Orange County, and at the cocktail party afterward one of the Mensa members came running up excitedly (this was during Barry Bonds's historic march to break the McGwire record) and announced that Bonds had gone deep twice that night. I said, "Must be nice for Mrs. Bonds."

TIPS

- Try and do a few wordplay jokes in a row so one doesn't sit there by itself.
- Remember, as your friend is speaking and unknowingly setting you up, flip the file cards in your head to get all the associations and references.
- Keep it short and snappy.
- Much of wordplay involves double entendres. Words like: play ball, hoe, bush, and my all-time favorite, Beaver College.

WARNING: Sprinkle these in occasionally or they get tiresome.

THE POINT TO REMEMBER

You need to walk and chew gum to use these effectively; in other words, LISTEN and think.

YOUR HOMEWORK ASSIGNMENT

1. *Hugh Hefner is giving a commencement speech at your local college. Find words that deal with college that you can associate with someone like Hugh Hefner.*

2. *Pretend you just split up with your wife. Or dump her, see if I care. A friend asks you if it's been a painful separation. Fill in the blank. "No, —— was a painful separation."*

Association

"Dino de Laurentiis is eighty years old. Or as Anna Nicole Smith calls him—fresh meat."
—Steve Martin

Association is the technique of combining two nonrelated items in a new way to create something unique and funny. In wordplay, you are associating similar words to the key word; in association, you are free-forming, letting your mind bring together two seemingly different concepts.

EXAMPLE: At that giant 9/11 benefit concert in New York at Madison Square Garden, Billy Crystal told the crowd this: "We all have our differences, but there is one thing we can all agree on whether we are Christian, Jewish, or Muslim. We can never again let Mariah Carey make another movie."

My Experience

Movie association is actually an easy and effective way to get a laugh. Movie titles are great because they are a well-known pop culture reference and all you need to do is associate something else out there with the current hit du jour.

I did this in a college lecture a few years ago to show how it can be done. I had the class throw out movie titles while I did a quick association, complaining that movie titles are confusing. Here is what I did.

MOVIE	ASSOCIATION
DIE HARD	I thought it was the story of Viagra.
ICE AGE	Who wants to hear about Frank and Kathie Lee's honeymoon?
WHAT WOMEN WANT	In L.A., a Porsche and some Botox.

TIPS

- Let your mind wander and connect the unrelated.
- It's always a good idea to work off something fresh in the pop culture, like a movie title or song.

WARNING: There is none.
This is my favorite technique.

THE POINT TO REMEMBER

Let your mind free-form concepts.

YOUR HOMEWORK ASSIGNMMENT

1. *Go to the movie page and make a list of ten movies at the theaters.*

2. *Associate something with the title.*

The Reverse

"I will not make age an issue in this campaign. I will not exploit my opponent's relative youth and inexperience."

—Ronald Reagan

"I just hope my getting this award finally opens the door for Jewish people trying to break into show business."

—Brad Garrett

. . . .

"The most important thing to succeed in show business is sincerity. And if you can fake that, you've got it made."

—George Burns

The reverse can involve any number of things: adding an opposite or incongruous punch line; flipping words or a situation; turning around and playing with the listener's beliefs. Jay Leno told a great joke about American Taliban fighter John Walker Lindh: "One day you're fighting to oppress women, the next day you're in prison and you are an oppressed woman."

EXAMPLES: A few years ago I was writing the American Comedy Awards and George Schlatter, Dave Boone, and I came up with a bit for Steve Harvey. He came onstage and started talking about the need for diversity in television, about how the industry was falling far short of its goals. He then said he had a problem finding qualified white people for his own show. He said he went everywhere, the country clubs, the

golf courses, the boardrooms, but it was just
so hard to find white people who could handle
the job.

Another example is from Rita Rudner: "My very first joke was I broke up with my boyfriend. He wanted to get married. I didn't want him to."

I've told Rita this is one of my all-time-favorite jokes. She believes it's an effective joke because as she puts it, "It doesn't pivot until the very end of the sentence, and *to* is such a tiny word that the U-turn is abrupt." This also adds the key element of surprise.

A third example of a reverse is a joke about the time that the Seattle lawyer had sex with her client in prison, a convicted murderer. That had to be creepy. Imagine having sex with a lawyer.

My Experience

Here are a few reverses I've used:

"He's good to all his children. Even the legitimate ones."

"He never forgot where he came from. That's because he's under house arrest."

"She's a perfect ten. If you like that sort of IQ."

TIPS

- The idea in a reverse is you want to switch the audience's point of view.
- Do not overplay the setup.

THE POINT TO REMEMBER

You need to use a reverse with a relatively high IQ audience. If your listener isn't smart enough to get the first part of the joke, he will never get the punch line.

YOUR HOMEWORK ASSIGNMENT

1. *Think of a stereotype, something like "Doctors are males," "There are no white guys in the NBA," "All women fake orgasms." Turn it into a joke.*

2. *Tell a joke about yourself and a person or situation that "fools" your listener.*

The Deliberate Misdirect

"The big story continues to be that she's blond, she's outrageous, and she doesn't get why people are laughing at her TV show. But enough about Martha Stewart."

—Jay Leno

Why did this joke work? Because at the time that Jay told it, everyone was talking about the first episode of the *Anna Nicole Show*.

The deliberate misdirect is an excellent way to begin a speech because it draws your audience in with a false premise, then switches it on them with a surprise. It is a more sophisticated form of a reverse.

> EXAMPLE: Let's say you are introducing Bob Wright, chairman of NBC, to a group of television reporters at the presentation of the new fall NBC lineup. These reporters are aware that Bob Wright is the boss and also know that NBC's schedule is flooded with *Law and Order* spin-offs from producer Dick Wolf. The audience knows you are there to introduce Bob Wright and so they are expecting some glowing words about him. Here is the misdirect:

> "I was asked here to introduce the man responsible for making NBC what it is today, a man with total control over the network, the one power at NBC who determines what shows will live and what will die. Unfortunately, Dick Wolf could not be here. So instead...here is Bob Wright."

In addition to using a misdirect in a speech, it is a great technique to use to open the day's conversation at work, especially when everyone is thinking and talking about the same giant story in the news.

My Experience

Last summer when everyone was talking about the rescue of those trapped Pennsylvania miners, I began every conversation by talking about how we had all gone to sleep fearing the worst and we all woke up to witness a miracle...Angelina Jolie finally left Billy Bob.

TIPS

- I like to set them up with a triple.
- With the misdirect (and all forms of the reverse), you need a smart audience that has a preconceived notion of where you are going and a body of knowledge about the event you are referring to or what hot topics are in the news.

THE POINT TO REMEMBER

Misdirects are a great way to begin a speech or public remarks to a group.

YOUR HOMEWORK ASSIGNMENT

1. *Pretend you have to introduce your boss or teacher to an audience at work or school.*

2. *Prepare a misdirect about someone other than your target that the audience would be familiar with.*

Storytelling

Probably the best style of being funny is to create your own story. Take a real incident from your life, embellish, exaggerate, and twist it so that it's funny.

"To be funny, go the opposite way of boasting. You want to play the game of 'Can you bottom this?'"

—Carrie Fisher

....

"Tell a story that is self-deprecating and involves some calamity about yourself."

—Bob Ellison

....

"The elements to a good story have been the same since the dawn of time. Setup, confrontation or situation, resolution, also known as the beginning, middle, and end."

—James Carville

....

"Telling a story is always better than telling jokes."

—Jay Leno

"My favorite storytellers, Bill Cosby, Louie Anderson, and Jay Leno, always draw a vivid picture
while they work . . . good details, language com-
mand, good acting, they use their voice and
there's a use of voices. The bad storyteller says
to an audience after bombing, 'You had to be
there.' The good storyteller makes you think you
were there."

—Arsenio Hall

Back to Andy Breckman, the creator of *Monk*. Andy's theory on how to be funny in everyday conversation is this:
"When you want to tell a story, try and remember the last
time you were embarrassed. When you tell an embarrassing moment, which is what *Seinfeld* was built on, you're
sharing something that 80 percent of the people can identify with. Every guy who spills water on his pants in the
men's room reacts the same way. He tries to dry it with the
hand dryer so that everyone doesn't think he wet himself.
So if you tell that story to people, they will identify with it."

EXAMPLE: Think about every routine Richard
Pryor or Bill Cosby has ever done.

Buz Kohan's wife, Rhea, told a great story when she was
the emcee at a charity luncheon. She told the audience
about going to the dentist and he kept asking her to open
wider. She said, "If I could open wider I'd have better
jewelry."

My Experience

I told this story on my weekly gig on the "Paul Harris Show" on KTRS in St. Louis after a friend of mine and his new girlfriend took me to a Moroccan restaurant. Remember, it's not funny to tell friends that the restaurant was good and that you had a great time. That changes you from being a funny person and turns you into a food critic. Funny is when there is a disaster and a victim—in this case, me:

I met an old buddy of mine and his new girlfriend for dinner, so of course I want to know how they met. She says they met on the Internet even though they are GU. How did I know GU is Internet for "geographically unfit"? I thought it meant gynecologically unfit. So now there's dead silence in the car when we go to this Moroccan restaurant. First thing the waiters do is make you put your hands over the table while they pour water over them. They're a very advanced culture. Up to the advanced part of the fourteenth century. And they were just thrilled when the Jew asks if this is how they make soup. So now the waiter is muttering in Moroceese and he puts a towel over my lap. That's how you wipe your hands after dipping into a pile of rancid hummus. I don't know what it's for; the last time I had a towel on my lap was at an adult theater. God, are they sensitive if you touch yourself after the appetizer. Finally they bring out the food. Excellent, if you like goat. So we're all dipping our hands in the goat stew when I have to go to the men's room. I go in, wash my hands, this time with actual soap, and there's a sign over the sink that says, "Employees must wash their hands before returning to work." It's never good when they have to remind the hired help that E. coli is a problem. Second, how about a sign about customers having to wash their hands? It's not the employees dipping their fingers into the goat pot pie, it's the people you're with. So I'm back at the table and I remember a study that says one out of two guys don't wash their hands in the bathroom. I know I washed my hands, which means my buddy is the other guy. So now I've completely lost my appetite, the waiter is still muttering about the Zionist scum who made a crack about hygiene, so I try to lighten the mood by saying, "And you wonder why Morocco leads the world in dysentery." I'm now the first person ever evicted from a restaurant with a guy yelling *jihad* at me.

TIPS

- What you do every day is the basis for a good story.
- You can tell a story every single Monday morning of your life when someone at school or work or at the Starbucks asks, "So what did you do this weekend?"
- Once you have a good story, build on it, perfect it, and use it each time you are with a new audience. These work extremely well on first dates.
- And now a tip from Carrie Fisher: "Some people see something and say, how awful. If you can see the absurdity and make it funny, it's a great story."

WARNING: When you start, keep your stories short.

"The best story is one that rambles on with no point and offends as many people as possible."

—Eddie Driscoll

(Note Eddie's use of sarcasm.)

THE POINT TO REMEMBER

To have a good story you need to be observant.

> # YOUR HOMEWORK ASSIGNMENT
>
> **1.** *Go out tonight.*
>
> **2.** *Observe people around you (in everyday situations).*
>
> **3.** *Make up a story and tell it tomorrow morning.*

Analogy

"President Bush talking about cleaning up corporate corruption is like P. Diddy endorsing gun control."

—Jon Macks

Yep, I just put in my own joke: "That's like Prince Charles claiming he got his job on merit." Analogy is in fact the "that's like." These are formulaic funny lines but can be effective. Analogy jokes are always useful as a way to comment on an event while watching TV or in the office when a rival or rival company needs to be put down.

EXAMPLE: Let's say you're from Ernst & Young and someone mentions that Arthur Andersen is pushing for cleaning up the corporate accounting rules. This is a perfect situation for something like: "Arthur Andersen talking about reform is like Star Jones giving diet tips."

My Experience

I sit on the boards of a number of youth sports organizations and invariably, at least once a year at a meeting, a well-known hothead will complain about the need to control the parents at a game. I usually handle this with a "Bob giving us advice on out-of-control parents is like Nick Nolte giving out grooming tips. What's next, tolerance lessons from Trent Lott?"

TIPS

- Don't overuse this technique. It's good once in a while to make a point.
- If you're going to be in a public setting, prepare your analogy in advance.

WARNING: No warning here other than to make your reference topical.

THE POINT TO REMEMBER

Just use the two key words—"that's like."

YOUR HOMEWORK ASSIGNMENT

1. *Listen to the radio on the way to work and choose a public figure for your analogy who has done something idiotic.*

2. *Prepare your analogy to spring on someone at an opportune moment during the day.*

Physical Humor

This is a short section because it's not easy to describe physical humor in a book.

The late great Sir Isaac Newton once came up with the scientific theory that "physical humor works in an inverse ratio to a person's age." He then got a huge laugh from fellow scientists by getting hit on the head with an apple.

There is nothing funnier to an eight-year-old than blowing milk out of a straw at lunch, yet oddly, that same sort of humor doesn't work on a date.

So as a general rule, once you get past the age of fourteen, skip all physical humor in everyday conversation unless you are a pro. Lighting a fart works for Adam Sandler; it will not work during a speech to your company board of directors.

3.

Proactive and Reactive Humor in Everyday Conversation

The Basic Tenets of Everyday Humor

What do you need to be funny in everyday conversation? Jeffrey Ross says that to be a professional comic, all you need is a sport jacket and a bad childhood, so I'll suggest to the amateur, all you need is the bad childhood...plus the tips in this book.

This section is designed to help you be funny in the conversations that make up your everyday routine. To be funny in everyday conversation, you have to understand the difference between proactive humor and reactive humor. With proactive humor, you think about the social situation you are about to enter and plan in advance what you want to say that's funny. You have, in essence, prepared stories or ad-libs. You anticipate a social situation and then the moment something occurs to trigger your prepared comment, you deliver the comment, establishing yourself as a person to whom everyone should listen. What I'm saying is, that if you want to be funny, you have to put in a little effort.

A classic example of a proactive line is the vice-presidential debate on October 5, 1988, between Lloyd Bentsen and Dan Quayle. Quayle tried to compare himself with John Kennedy by mentioning that he had as much experience in the Congress as Jack Kennedy did when he sought the presidency. Senator Bentsen's response: "Senator, I served with Jack Kennedy, I knew Jack Kennedy, Jack Kennedy was a friend of mine. Senator, you are no Jack Kennedy."

Great spontaneous line, right? Wrong. The Bentsen people knew that Quayle had been using that line in speeches around the country the week before the debate so they prepared a triple. It was sitting in Bentsen's memory storage file, waiting to be delivered at the right moment. Although it seems reactive, the truth is it was prepared in advance, and by my definition that's proactive humor.

Remember, a "spontaneous" ad-lib by one of the comic greats is the result of either knowing in advance what could happen and being prepared to act, or, in the split second they hear a key word or premise, rifling through the mental file cards and instantly retrieving and delivering a line that has been waiting there in storage. It's like the concept of improv. All the great improv comics are just accessing what's already in the file, and selecting a response—or file card—accordingly.

Think of your mind as a huge dictionary. All of us have the same words in storage. Funny people are 1) able to reassemble those words quickly to say something funny and 2) more important, are willing to reassemble those words in storage to say something funny. And anyone can do it—face it, put a monkey at a computer and eventually he will randomly type something funny. It's very similar to Andy Dick and Tom Green.

Reactive humor in everyday conversation involves three basic steps: listening to what the other person is saying, associating something in your memory file with a key word, and delivering the comment. If one was to give a percentage of proactive humor versus reactive humor, I'd say that in speeches and presentations it's 95 percent proactive, but in everyday conversation, 60 to 70 percent of what you do is reactive comedy.

Reactive comedy is not only important for you. It's the latest trend in television. Great sitcoms like *Curb Your Enthusiasm* don't even use written scripts. Instead, Larry David writes a five-page outline, which he doesn't share with the actors until the day of shooting. He gives the cast a general idea of what is to happen in each scene but doesn't tell them what he is going to say. They have to react to him and play off his dialogue.

If you watch *Hollywood Squares,* you'll see that every joke is reactive. Question from Tom Bergeron, joke by the star. Take a look at one of the shows (actually, take a look at all the shows because the more you watch, the more money I can make) and see how stars like Martin Mull, Ellen DeGeneres, and Howie Mandel key off a word in the question to launch their jokes.

How does this work for those of you who are not yet on *Hollywood Squares*?

EXAMPLE: You're standing in line at a Burger King. The attractive and surprisingly pimple-free person at the counter asks, "Is there anything else I can get you?" The key word in that sentence is *get,* so you can quickly react with something from the eleven types of humor listed in Chapter 2.

BURGER KING EMPLOYEE: Is there something else I can get you?
YOU: How about a toupee that doesn't look so fake?

So, whether you are the Fred Astaire of the conversation (being proactive) or the Ginger Rogers and following the lead (reactive), here are the ten commandments to follow to be funny in everyday conversation.

The 10 Commandments

1. *Decide you want to be funny.*

2. *Read a newspaper and know what's going on in the world.*

3. *Listen to what people are saying and be able to think in the moment.*

4. *Key in on a word they use as your jumping-off point.*

5. *Associate with that key word.*

6. *Have some stock transitional phrases that enable you to buy time as you search for the reference and connect to the point you're going to make: "There's a great idea." "I'm shocked." "Now let me get this straight."*

7. *Rifle through prepared ad-libs.*

8. *Remember your building blocks of being funny: See the 13 Rules in Chapter 20.*

9. *When in doubt, always say the opposite of what's expected.*

10. *Don't let a lack of a laugh deter you. Be confident. You're funny, they're not.*

Now, let's learn how to use these in everyday conversation situations.

COMMON CONVERSATIONS
IN WHICH YOU WANT TO BE FUNNY

CONVERSATION SITUATION 1

PICKING UP A GUY, A GIRL, OR BOTH

Proactive Pickup Humor

This is not a collection of stock pickup lines. These are ways to impress a member of the opposite or same sex with your wit and charm. There are two ways to do this: one is "in the moment" humor; second is through storytelling (see Chapter 2). With "in the moment" comedy, you are observing right then your collective situation, finding something unique about it, and commenting. This bonds you with your target audience, and if they react to your line, it can lead to actual conversation...and if it doesn't work out, at least it gives you a funny story. Look, if you're rich or built like a Chippendale dancer, you don't need conversation.

SUGGESTION FOR GAYS (for we are nothing if we are not inclusive): You're at a concert sitting

74

next to a very attractive guy. You see someone
walk by in a military uniform. You turn to the person of interest and say, "I was going to be in the
army but they asked, I told."

Reactive Pickup Humor

At this point, you are keying in on something your tar-
geted love interest has said to you. As always, find a
word and key in on it to tell a story or two. This does
not, repeat, *does not* mean using stupid pickup lines.
Those are too obvious. Just be funny.

> You're at a wedding and the bridesmaid comes up
> to you and says the following...(since she's a
> bridesmaid, it's already a sure thing so you don't
> even need to talk, just point to a nearby closet.
> But just in case...)

BRIDESMAID: So how do you know Jimmy?
YOU: As a parole officer, I stay in touch with all
my boys.

That was a good example. Here is a bad example.

BRIDESMAID: Do you know what time it is?
YOU: Time for you to climb on my leg.

If you insist on trying a pickup line, I suggest using something nonsexual and something so outrageously stupid that if he or she has any sense of humor, they'll laugh.

Guys, try something in a run: "So, who's your favorite Friend? Mine's Matt, but sometimes it's Matthew. Is it just me that Dr. Phil makes cry? Do these pants make my butt look big?"

Women, try something sports related but outrageous: "Is it just me or do you think Janet Reno should be tested for steroids?"

And you know something? If they don't laugh, they're not worth dating.

YOUR HOMEWORK ASSIGNMENT

1. *Go out tonight and pick up someone with a funny line.*

2. *If you're married, do it anyway and claim it's part of your homework.*

CONVERSATION SITUATION 2

DATING

"If you want to put someone at ease on a date, highlight a flaw in yourself. If you have a big nose, if you're fat, or if you're poor, you might refer to it. Although if those three things apply, I'm not sure how you got a date."

—Rita Rudner

Proactive Date Humor

Being funny on a date does not mean seeing *Goldmember* and endlessly repeating on the way home, "Do I make you horny, baby?" Being funny on a date means taking the same techniques you used to meet your little love muffin and using them to bond. Make fun of the traffic, talk about work and your family or mutual strange friends. Tell stories, embellish and exaggerate. If you spend thirty minutes before the date picking out the right restaurant, the best movie, and the hottest clothes, if you spend an hour grooming and showering, why not spend ten minutes thinking about interesting and funny topics of conversation? In the last chapter you worked on developing a funny story; now is the time to tell it.

SUGGESTION: Talk to your date about siblings or family. When you mention your recently divorced sister with two kids, don't say she has relationship problems. Say she's in Chicago to tape a whole week of *Springer* because your family wants to have her spayed to keep her from spawning another defective generation of redneck trash.

(Note the use of funny words. "Spawning" is much funnier than "having kids.")

Or talk to your date about your job. Men, no bragging about how successful you are, and women, no whining about how the other women at work are so mean to you. Instead, tell your date a funny story about a client, a case, a customer.

> QUICK COMEDY NOTE: Yes, you have to work at being funny. You have to think and read and make a concerted effort to say funny things.

Looking for something to talk about?

> **"Just remember, everyone's mother is weird."**
> **—Carrie Fisher**

And now some comedy advice from *Hollywood Squares* head writer and dating-comedy expert Dave Boone.

> **"The key to being funny on a date is to never *try*
> to be funny. The best thing to do is to be natural
> and self-deprecating. Women, in my experience,
> love to laugh. Okay, sometimes they laugh at the
> wrong times, but there are pills for that now.
> Always use yourself as the target. Too many
> times I've fallen into the trap of believing that a**

girl had a great sense of humor and then screwed everything up by turning my sights on her. Her eye shadow, her outfit, the piece of spinach lodged in her eyebrow—all bad things to talk about. If you have a clever wit for making fun of people's outfits, talk about something you've worn that you couldn't pull off, or the people at the next table. Women love to laugh at others, but stay away from physical attributes and don't come off too mean. You never know if the pear-shaped fat guy in the corner booth is actually two sizes smaller than her mother. Be natural, and if you happen to make a joke she doesn't get, don't over-explain it. Never make her feel bad or inferior because she didn't get your reference. It might be possible that you weren't that funny in the first place. Find the things she likes to laugh at and stay within those boundaries until you get to know each other better."

Reactive Date Humor

Unlike that of a pickup situation, in which you are being a more aggressive talker, dating humor tends to be more reactive as it involves listening. This is relatively easy for women. Guys, you have to move beyond the step of pretending to listen and actually listen. Think of it this way: if you can listen for a few minutes and find a key word to react to, you can then talk and actually be funny.

But here is a practical warning from Carrie Fisher: "On a date I would caution you from telling a story that makes you seem weird. Don't say anything that would stop them from sleeping with you."

SUGGESTION: You and your date are trying to decide what movie to rent. She wants to see *Stuart Little 2* because she thinks it would be cute. You want to see *American Pie 2* because it has juvenile humor and bare breasts.

You can't very well win this argument by saying *Pie* is one of the American Film Institute's classic one hundred films of all time, or that it is a serious exposé of the dark side of college. So...pick up on a key word and react, putting down her choice in an amusing way while leaving your movie as the only option.

DATE: Let's rent *Stuart Little 2,* he's so cute.
YOU: The word *little* causes guys a real psychological problem. Bob Dole saw the first *Stuart Little,* two days later he was a Viagra spokesman.

Or

"If mice and vermin [funny word alert!] are so cute, how come people climb on chairs to get away from them?"

YOUR HOMEWORK ASSIGNMENT

1. *Go out on a date.*

2. *Listen to something your date says.*

3. *React to the key word with an association joke or wordplay.*

CONVERSATION SITUATION 3

WORKING OUT

Proactive Gym Humor

A fitness and health club is a great place to be funny because there are so many things to make fun of: sweaty equipment, strange body parts, implants, bald account-ants with weight-lifter belts, camel toes (and if you don't know what a camel toe is, go to www.cameltoe.org), los-ers who really don't work out but are just there to be seen. The other great advantage of being funny at the health club is the more you're talking, the less you are actually working out and inflicting pain on your body.

> EXAMPLE: My trainer is named Josh. Young guy, about twenty-four. I make my workout with him

bearable by, without being asked, giving him advice on women. Remember: Good advice isn't funny. Bad, outrageous advice is funny. So I give him the worst advice possible. I describe marriage as a living hell, how his girlfriend will undoubtedly trap him in an unloving relationship and saddle him with a brood of kids. I let him know that her firm, tight twenty-three-year-old body within weeks of marriage will become a mountain of sagging flesh and that post-honeymoon, the best sex he'll ever have is when his wife pretends to be asleep and he humps her leg. That is marriage.

Reactive Gym Humor

Most humor at the gym is reactive. But your setup isn't necessarily a word said by someone; it may be your reaction to something you see.

EXAMPLE: This actually happened to me. I was at the gym and right after working out I was in line to get a protein shake. Standing in front of me was Jose Canseco. It was the week he had revealed his steroid use and everyone in line was staring at him but trying not to look. He got his smoothie, paid, and the second he left I said, "Look, he's injecting it into his buttocks. It's the number five special, pineapple and anabolics."

YOUR HOMEWORK ASSIGNMENT

1. *Join a health club/go to your health club.*

2. *Work out.*

3. *Make fun of the person next to you the minute he or she is out of hearing range.*

CONVERSATION SITUATION 4

ELEVATOR CONVERSATION

Proactive Elevator Humor

No one talks in an elevator. I'm sure there is some deep reason, related to our subconscious ancestral memory of being in the cave when saber-toothed tigers roamed the earth, but that's no excuse in the year 2003 not to try some humor. An elevator is the perfect place to be funny because no one expects it, there's a nervous audience, and one word from you puts you in charge. Plus if a joke dies, there are only a few seconds before the audience or you leave, never to be seen again.

You want to say something that plays on everyone being ill at ease in a claustrophobia-inducing mechanical device.

SUGGESTED LINES (Try these out and then come up with your own.)

NOTE: It's always good to be on the elevator with a friend/comic foil you can deliver this to so that the other passengers don't have you committed.

NOTE 2: After each line, there is a quick explanation of why it works.

"Does anyone have Dramamine?" (use of funny word)

"Is it me or are elevators the perfect place for a first date?" (sarcasm)

"Is that a chalk body outline in the corner?" (shock value)

"I swear, I'm going to beat this indictment." (surprise/deadpan delivery/funny word at end)

"It's working better since the accident." (saying the opposite)

"Is it buy low, sell high, or buy high, sell low?" (a bit of wordplay)

"Underpants are way overrated." (use of a funny word)

"I'm thinking of marrying Jennifer Lopez." (current events reference)

Reactive Elevator Humor

In this case you are almost always reacting to a strange person who just left. My favorite is to wait until the bike messenger has gotten off at the eleventh floor and then say, "He used to be CEO of Enron."

EXAMPLE: The other day I was in the *Variety* building on Wilshire and a woman got on, a bit annoyed because she said she had to go back to her office because she forgot something. I said, "That's never happened to me, you must be the first person ever to forget something." It was a way of making her laugh at her situation.

YOUR HOMEWORK ASSIGNMENT

1. *Get a job in an office building.*

2. *Spend your lunch hour riding the elevator.*

3. *Say funny lines and keep the ones that work.*

4. *Quit your job as now people think you're a lunatic and start a new job with your freshly prepared great lines.*

CONVERSATION SITUATION 5

TALKING AT STARBUCKS

This may be the single most important thing I can teach you because approximately 30 percent of your life will be spent at Starbucks staring at the person's head in front of you in line, and not saying anything. Why not mine for gold in a gold mine? There are so many things to make fun of at Starbucks: people talking on cell phones, annoying kids, the word *barista*, head lice, the fact there are thirty of you in line paying $3.50 for a cup of coffee while people are starving in Somalia. In fact, there are supermodels starving right here in L.A.

Proactive Humor
Use the common bond that you have with the other seventy people in line to comment on the Starbucks experience. Let's be honest, it is funny that we're all paying so much for a sixty-cent cup of coffee.

You walk into Starbucks and there are twenty people in line paying $3.60 for a latte.

Your reaction: "That's what I love about California. People pay $3.60 for a 12-ounce latte but complain when gas is $1.80 a gallon."

Reactive Humor

You want to use the natural separation of the line shuffling to the counter to make yourself the head of your group, by reacting to what someone in the other group says or does.

In every Starbucks, there is a soccer mom in spandex talking on her cell phone, rifling through her purse while her screaming litter of childlike animals are rampaging through the store. Catch the eye of someone who is also staring at this scene in horror and say, "Note to self, get a vasectomy," or, "Note to self, get tubes tied."

YOUR HOMEWORK ASSIGNMENT

1. *Refinance your house.*

2. *Save $300 a month.*

3. *Use the money to go to Starbucks for a month and perfect your lines.*

CONVERSATION SITUATION 6

TALKING TO SALES CLERKS

Your goal in being funny at the mall is to bond with a $4.50-an-hour slug of a young Gen-Y sales clerk so that helping you, their funny new friend, becomes their number-two top priority, right after scoring some Ecstasy for the weekend rave.

Proactive Humor
Find something in the store to focus on and make fun of: the lighting, the boss, the lack of air-conditioning. Another idea is to just give a nice opening line before getting to your problem.

SUGGESTED LINES TO TRY

"Before I even tell you what I need, I've already talked to your boss. I'm recommending a huge raise for you, consider it done."

"Do you want me to get your boss a pamphlet on sweat-shops?"

"Is Scrooge still your boss?"

Reactive Humor

The best approach is to make fun of the annoying customer who was right before you. You want to bond with your salesperson by targeting the previous customer as the idiot.

SUGGESTED LINES TO TRY
(Use these to refer to the obnoxious person in line in front of you.)

"He reminds me of my old prison guard."

"Next time he comes in, I'll have Prozac and a tranquilizer dart."

"He seems so lifelike."

"Three letters—P-M-S."

YOUR HOMEWORK ASSIGNMENT

1. *Take the $7 you have remaining from your home refinancing and trip to Starbucks.*

2. *Go to the mall.*

3. *Make the salesperson laugh.*

> **4.** *Optional—go to a Hertz center and make fun of the rental agreement and your eyesight.*

CONVERSATION SITUATION 7

ARGUING WITH YOUR SPOUSE

Can being funny help you end an argument with your spouse? Yes, at times it can. And even if it doesn't, it's better than the Robert Blake solution.

Proactive Humor
What you want to do here is to change the subject. You especially want to do this when you are losing the argument.

> SUGGESTION: No matter what the fight is about, just suck it up and say, "I am so lucky to be married to you. Can you imagine the nightmare if I had married Cindy? Her ass has its own zip code. She's so ugly, after sex I'd take roofies so I'd forget."

This will immediately get your wife focusing on the size of Cindy's ass, the fact that she and Cindy had a huge argument two weeks ago, or, if Cindy and your wife have now made up, your wife will then try to convince you Cindy is really her best friend, thereby forgetting the reason the two of you were fighting.

> SUGGESTION FOR WOMEN: Women who want to end arguments with their husbands don't necessarily need to be funny, they need to change the subject by bringing up the last funny thing their husbands said, repeating it back, and telling them how funny they are.
>
> Remember—when women say they want to be with someone funny, they mean they want someone to make them laugh; when men say they want to be with someone funny, they want someone to laugh at what they say.

So the rules for ending a fight with your spouse are:

1. *Find a target—her friend, his boss.*

2. *Compliment the person you're fighting with and tag the compliment with a joke about the target.*

3. *Pretend you're French and immediately surrender.*

4. *When in doubt, there's nothing better than makeup sex.*

This last step is true—according to the latest study, one in three arguments ends when the two participants have sex. Which is going to make for some pretty exciting presidential debates.

Reactive Humor

You want to use this when you are winning the argument. At this point, you are finding a key word, making a joke, and letting your opponent focus on that as his graceful way out. One effective way to do that is to deliberately misunderstand something he said.

> EXAMPLE: This actually happened with my wife and me. For once she was actually losing an argument with me so she tried to change the subject.
>
> SHE: Calm down. I need to get you a yoga instructor.
> HE: Yogurt? Why do I need a yogurt instructor? Look, I didn't go to public schools, I know how to eat yogurt. You shake up the container, open the top, and then eat. Open the top first and then shake it and you have a mess. Hire the yogurt instructor for someone else.

1. *Get married.*

2. *Pick a fight with your spouse.*

3. *End it. (Either the fight or the marriage.)*

CONVERSATION SITUATION 8

TALKING TO YOUR TEEN

"As a father, I can't think of a device that has served me greater than humor. Whether it's making a tense, awkward moment lighter or making a boring bedtime story an incredible epic, humor rules the world of parenting."

—Arsenio Hall

You will want to have two types of conversations with your teenager. The first will be when you are trying to prove a point about yourself—that you're smart or "with it" or that you care. The second will be when you are trying to make a point about something he or she is wearing, or planning to do—in essence, a reactive conversation.

Proactive Humor

In telling you how to be funny talking to your teen, this is more of a series of don'ts. Don't try and be cool. Don't talk to him about sex; it's creepy, especially since he knows more than you. And don't tell him about how successful you were when you were his age. He won't believe it and chances are, you're lying anyway.

> SUGGESTIONS: **Make yourself the victim.** Tell a story with you as the fool. One, they'll laugh; two, they might just possibly remember it when they have done something stupid and it will make them feel better about their miserable acne- and angst-ridden adolescence.

My kids still throw this one back at me and actually laugh at it so it must have worked. I once told them the story of my first baseball game. I was six, and my very first at-bat, I hit a shot deep to left field. I had no idea what to do until the parents yelled at me to run to first. When I got there I stopped. The same thing happened: they yelled at me to run to second and then third. At that point the outfielder had picked up the ball and everyone told me to "run home." So I ran the three blocks to my house. True story.

Reactive Humor

Sarcasm is the only way to go with your teen. The beauty is that it's not aimed at him so he won't even know you're being sarcastic. You're using him to get a laugh from your spouse or other adults or kids present, with the added bonus that it may actually make a point.

For example, you're a mom and your daughter walks downstairs to breakfast, which she will not eat anyway, with pink spiked hair, a nose ring, and a skirt that is flashing "I'm easy." It will not work to order her not to wear this. It may just work if you use sarcasm. Tell her how great she looks; you saw Kelly Osbourne wearing the same thing and all the other moms your age think Kelly is really cool and (you have to use this phrase) "the bomb." Praise the look for about fifteen minutes and then tell her you plan to get the same thing. Suggest that the two of you go out and get matching nipple rings. Your daughter will be back to normal by the afternoon.

HOMEWORK ASSIGNMENT

1. *Think of a story in which you are the idiot.*

2. *Share it with your kids.*

CONVERSATION SITUATION 9

TALKING TO YOUR PARENTS (IF YOU'RE A TEEN)

There are special rules for teenagers who are trying to have conversations with their parents. First of all, the rule of storytelling does not apply to you when the audience is your parents. Never, ever, ever tell them exaggerated funny stories from your life. It will scare them to death. Second, don't make jokes about sex. They may try and share something about their sex lives and it's just too horrible to contemplate because you will then have visions of their ancient, intermingled flesh.

Proactive Humor

As a teen you have a critical need to be funny in a proactive conversation when you want something. Use humor to pretend you care about your parents and to show you have not cut off all contact with them. Yet.

The key is to make a joke about something in the news. This will impress them that you are smart, demonstrate you are funny, and then as they sit there shocked, you can hit them with your request. Here's an example:

TEEN: I saw in the news that President Bush wants to invade Iraq. I'm not going to believe we're going to war until I see him join the Texas National Guard.
PARENT: That's really funny. And smart.
TEEN: Can I have a new Lexus?

Reactive Humor

This is similar to the way your parents use reactive humor with you, except your use of sarcasm will be instantly noticed.

Let's say you and your friends are at the mall and you see Mom wearing a too short skirt and your three-year-old 'N SYNC RULES T-shirt that you thought was cool back in 2000. Introduce her to your friends by saying, "This is my mom, she's a Christina Aguilera wanna be." This sarcasm will do three things: 1) get a big laugh from your friends; 2) make an important point about not acting fifteen to your mom; and 3) get you grounded for a week. But if you want to be funny, the laugh is worth it.

YOUR HOMEWORK ASSIGNMENT

1. *Watch the news for fifteen minutes.*

2. *Find out where your parents eat their meals and join them.*

3. *Say something funny about what you saw on the news.*

4. *Ask for new Lexus.*

CONVERSATION SITUATION 10

CARPOOLING AND COMMUTING

Obviously this does not apply to L.A. because no one here has ever carpooled or taken public transportation. But whether on the train, the bus, or in a car during the morning commute, you can make the ride a hell of a lot better by being the funny person. Not only that, when everyone gets to work, they will spread the news that you are funny.

Proactive Humor
The car is a key place to try out your weekend story. You will only want to do this in a car, not on a bus or the Amtrak Metroliner because if you start babbling there,

people will think you are a deranged psychotic. Inevitably in the carpool, someone will ask what you did over the weekend. Now is the time to unleash your story or give a line about the big news event of the morning.

Reactive Humor

This can be used in the car or on public transportation. You can react to some music on the radio, which gives you a good chance to work on your association; you can comment about something on the all-news radio station; you can listen to what someone else is saying and do a play on words; it's also a good way to make fun of other drivers or, on public transportation, to cut the nut from the herd after he gets off at his stop.

Let's say a classic rock station is on and you hear the song "19th Nervous Breakdown." Your comment: "I thought '19th Nervous Breakdown' was about [fill in name of a coworker]."

Or you see a crazed driver zigzagging in and out of lanes. Just mention "That's [fill in name of the most recent crazed celebrity driver—Halle Berry, Nick Nolte, Randy Moss, Diana Ross—don't worry, there's a new one every week]."

"One rule for a carpool: Don't make fun of the driver. You're better off dissing people in your old carpool."

—Paul Harris

YOUR HOMEWORK ASSIGNMENT

1. *Have a cup of coffee before your commute.*

2. *Listen to the radio while drinking that cup of coffee.*

3. *Make an association about what you heard.*

CONVERSATION SITUATION 11

ACCEPTING A COMPLIMENT

A lot of people out there have a hard time accepting a compliment. Not me, but I've heard this happens with others. The standard response to a compliment is to 1) deny it, which diminishes the pleasure of having received it and makes the person who gave you the compliment feel ill at ease or 2) not say a word.

How about acknowledging it with a joke? It shows you appreciate it and you're giving someone something in return—a laugh.

Reactive Humor
Obviously this is 100 percent reactive humor unless you're a schizophrenic narcissist who stares in the mir-

ror complimenting the other you. What you want to do is either react with a key word or use exaggeration.

Let's say someone compliments you on what great shape you're in. Just say, "Yeah, the new steroids are great."

Or, someone remarks that you look really sexy. Use the great Dolly Parton line that it takes a lot of money to look this cheap.

CONVERSATION SITUATION 12

BUSTING YOUR FRIENDS

Prostitution is the oldest profession; the oldest form of humor is sitting around with friends, male or female, and busting balls...or ovaries, as the case may be. I'm sure they were doing it sitting around the fire of the Stone Age cave, and it's the type of humor that can be the most fun. In fact, I bet that's why they call it a roast—the hunt was done, everyone came back safely to the cave and sat around a big cave fire, roasting a delicious mammoth tusk and busting one another. Remember, we always roast the ones we love best. Jeffrey Ross once told me there is nothing funnier than making fun of Uncle Murray eating. Since no one busts his friends better than Jeffrey, here is advice from the master.

Jeffrey Ross's 5 F's of Insult Humor

FAST: You want to be fast. You want to react quickly. You don't have to be the wittiest, if you say it the fastest.

FUNNY: Don't edit yourself. You're among friends. Say it. If you think it's funny, it is.

FIERCE: Go for the jugular.

FRIENDLY: But add a little sugar; remember you are with friends and family. I love my uncle Murray but the way he eats, you'd think he has two assholes.

FUCK*: Adding the word *fuck* among friends can help any insult. As in, "Nice tie, fuckface."

---

* Know your audience. With friends, dropping the "F" word is not bad language, it's funny. However, using the "F" word during a parent-teacher conference generally doesn't work. If you ever use it at an inappropriate time, simply mutter, "I have Tourette's syndrome," and chances are, your audience will nod sympathetically.

• •

PLAYING THE DOZENS

"Your mama's so fat when she cut her legs shaving gravy came out."

In the African-American community playing the dozens (aka snaps or ranking) is a much more formalized way of busting your friends. We know it best as "your mama"; in fact, the first "your mama" joke has its roots four hundred years ago in Shakespeare:

> "Thou clay brained guts, thou knotty pated fool,
> thou whoreson, obscene, greasy tallow catch."
> —*Henry IV, Part I*, **Act II, Scene iv**

For now we're talking about the fun busting of friends. Later on, we'll see how the same technique can be used to put down an enemy.

TIPS FOR PLAYING THE DOZENS

1. There are boxers and fighters. Boxers are quick; fighters deliver the big knockout blow.
2. The best targets are your friends, their family members, and people they're dating.
3. There's a standard setup: "your mama's so fat," "you're so dumb," "your mama is so ugly."
4. Be observant—know what your friend/opponent is wearing, who he's dating, what she looks like.

103

4.

Advice from the Pros—
The Comedy
Roundtable...
Without the Table

Simon & Schuster gave me an advance of $7,500 to take out some friends, writers and comics, to a series of dinners and record their comments as part of a comedy roundtable. The idea was that these pros—performers, producers, writers, and public speakers such as Jay Leno, Billy Crystal, Garry Shandling, Rita Rudner, Conan O'Brien, Arsenio Hall, Bruce Vilanch, Jeffrey Ross, Dave Barry, George Schlatter, Mary Matalin, James Carville, Carrie Fisher, Gilbert Gottfried, Dave Boone, Eddie Driscoll, Paul Harris, Buz Kohan, Stefanie Wilder, and Paul Begala—would have a great time and I would be able to collect their tips and advice to pass on to you.

Then I had a brilliant idea—keep the $7,500, use it as a down payment on a new Porsche, call these people up collect, get their tips for free, and then organize it as if they were all at dinner with me. I think it worked out pretty well.

> "My funny comes from the fact I think everything is absurd. If it's not funny, it just happened in your life. Be a spy in the house of you. You're on the frontline so you have to look at yourself and report."
>
> —Carrie Fisher

....

> "I really didn't ever think I was funny. I was very shy and didn't talk until I was twenty-two. I was boring. Whenever we played doctor, I was always the anesthesiologist. I struggle every day to try to write new jokes and always doubt my ability to do so. I think insecurity is a key to being funny."
>
> —Rita Rudner

....

> "I first realized I was funny when I was a kid. But that needn't stop you. It's never too late to discover the kid inside you, and that is the place

where you feel funny and from which the best humor comes."

—Garry Shandling

. . . .

"I was the one in school who was always piping up. And I always thought it was everyone else who was funny, but when your friends say that you're the funny one in the group, you start to think it might be true."

—Eddie Driscoll

. . . .

"I always used to say I used humor to defuse a situation when I was a kid but it was really just a way to get an extra minute to run away from danger. As an adult, it still is."

—Bruce Vilanch

. . . .

"It starts with your family when you first realize you're funny. When I was eight I played Abraham Lincoln in a school play. Seeing me onstage wearing a beard made everyone in my family laugh and their laughing made the audience laugh. I wasn't sure what I did that made that happen but I knew then I could make people laugh."

—Buz Kohan

"My first real joke was in the fourth-grade talent show. My friend Joel wrapped himself up in bandages like a mummy and held a sign that read '400 B.C.' I said that was the license plate of the car that ran over him."

—Jay Leno

....

"My father was a Baptist preacher. Going to work with Dad often meant going to funerals and weddings with him. One afternoon as I sat on the side, listening to Dad routinely guide another group of strangers through their vows, they got to the 'you may now kiss the bride.' The kiss went on forever, much longer than the kisses I was used to seeing. The couple became more aggressive and it started to look like a Tonya Harding honeymoon porno film. Well, I blurted out, 'Kiss her, don't kill her.' Because I was five years old and the timing was perfect, I got a huge laugh. I don't have to tell you what I got from my dad when I got home. But I didn't care. I was funny."

—Arsenio Hall

....

"The earliest I can remember being funny was back in kindergarten. The teacher was talking to the class while she was holding a newspaper; one kid wasn't listening so she walked up behind him and put a newspaper on his head. I said, 'Those are the headlines.'"

—Gilbert Gottfried

....

"As a little kid I always liked words, the way they sounded, what they meant, what you could make them mean. At some point some grown-up made the mistake of telling me a bunch of riddles that were full of puns and I loved every one of them. From that moment on, I started making up my own puns. It wasn't sophisticated stuff but when you're in elementary school and can make other kids giggle, it's magical."

—Paul Harris

....

"The first time I realized that I was funny was one day when my parents were having a big party. I sat down to play and everyone started laughing uproariously. How was I supposed to know that the bathroom door was open."

—George Schlatter

"The first time I remember being funny was when I was ten years old. I used to play basketball with three brothers who lived on my street. They were all good; I was the pudgy Jewish kid who couldn't play. I couldn't dribble, I'd always lose the ball, so every time I'd get it everyone would yell 'shoot, shoot,' figuring that it was better if the ball was in the air rather than in my hands. The score was ten to ten and the ball kept ending up in my hands. They were yelling at me to shoot so finally I just turned, pointed my finger, and yelled 'bang.' They all fell to the ground laughing; no one cared about the score and I got a laugh. It proved to me that when you're in a panic situation, being funny can get you out of it."

—Jeffrey Ross

....

"To be funny in everyday conversation, for someone who doesn't think of everything as absurd automatically like I do, visit your life as a Martian, and then as that Martian, tell people what happened to you that day."

—Carrie Fisher

"Avoid telling jokes from a joke book. Always try to speak with your own voice, personality, and thoughts, and if that fails, slip on a banana peel and fall down a manhole."

—Rita Rudner

. . . .

"Talking about your real experiences is always better than telling jokes. Keep it personal and come across as natural."

—Jay Leno

. . . .

"The cardinal rule on humor is to make it natural to your style. There is nothing worse than trying to sound like someone else or use a form of humor that makes you look uncomfortable."

—Mary Matalin

. . . .

"I laugh the hardest when someone creates something funny in front of me, spontaneously. I've never responded well to prepared jokes. They're too formal and linear. I love listening to people be funny off the top of their heads. There's nothing more exciting than being there at the moment of creation. And, I've noticed that audiences can always tell when you're being spontaneous. They always prefer the ad-libbed moment to any prepared joke. Spontaneity has an aura that people can detect. So, although it's important to prepare in comedy, I think people should leave plenty of room for improvisation."

—Conan O'Brien

....

"Sell the joke. If you think something is funny, deliver it. If it's funny, it will get a better laugh if you give it one hundred percent. Because if you lack confidence in a joke, the audience will know it right away. I think Henry Kissinger said that."

—Billy Crystal

....

"Say it with conviction. Know that it's funny and it will be."

—Stefanie Wilder

....

"If you want to learn to be funny, go to an AA meeting because the people there have to make fun of their life almost ending."

—Carrie Fisher

"Know your audience and talk about something
they know."

—Buz Kohan

....

"Remember that the audience *wants* you to be
funny, unless you're speaking at a funeral. And
even then, the audience is usually happy to hear
a joke. Because audiences expect to be bored.
Audiences spend most of their time waiting for
whatever it is to end. So when a speaker makes a
joke, even a semi-lame joke, the audience is
grateful for the diversion. Trust me on this: THEY
WANT HUMOR. So go ahead and try it, and as
long as your jokes are appropriate, I guarantee
you'll get a good response. (Tip: If you get gunfire, your jokes were not appropriate.)"

—Dave Barry

....

"The main thing I want to say, if it wasn't funny,
it would just be true."

—Carrie Fisher

....

"There's a saying that there's nothing funnier
than the truth. And that's true, although it
doesn't seem so funny right now. The only thing

funnier than the truth is a really good joke, but those are hard to come by. A small laugh from something true usually has more impact than a big laugh from, let's say, an old, classic joke. So go with what you have: a funny true story about a coworker beats an old joke, but if you've got a great joke, do it. If you have neither, sing. That will surely get a laugh."

—Garry Shandling

5

The Comedy Prescription:
What You Need to Do to Be Funny When You Really Need to Be Funny

1. How to Be a Funny Public Speaker

I'm starting with this one and will spend a dispropor-
tionate (compared with other sections) amount of time
on it because public speaking is the one area where people want and need the most help.

It has been said that the average American has three
great fears in life: death, taxes, and public speaking.
(Actually four great fears if you count the fear of waking
up next to Rosie O'Donnell.)

Death, only God can help you with. Taxes, even God
can't help you with. But public speaking, that's where I
can help. In addition to my work on *The Tonight Show*, I

write material for about two dozen elected officials, pro athletes, actors, actresses, and corporate CEO's, all of whom know that the key to making a good public speech is to get the audience on your side with a laugh.

First, some advice from the pros on giving a speech:

"Never say 'but seriously' after a joke doesn't work. Just move on to the next joke or the next part of your speech."

—Jay Leno

....

"The most important thing is to keep it short. I think more than ninety percent of the people who stand up and try to be funny end up going on too long. Know the gist of what you're going to say and give yourself a cutoff point. It's like knowing when to leave the table in Vegas. I always tell my writers that we've never had one letter complaining that a funny sketch should have gone on longer. Get your laugh or, if you're lucky, laughs, and then get the hell off the stage. If you don't trust yourself, hire a friend to tackle you after four minutes."

—Conan O'Brien

"A good rule of thumb is to cut every joke by fifty percent. And cut your expectations by that when you're speaking to an audience. If you have a great joke, count on a good laugh. If you expect a good laugh, count on a chuckle. If you expect a chuckle, count on a murmur, and if you expect a murmur, you'll get silence."

—Jay Leno

....

"If you're giving a speech, I would also raise your vulnerability level. Remember, there is nothing funny about a good-looking person doing well."

—Rita Rudner

....

"Generally when women give a speech, they can't tell jokes as well as men but are better at telling funny stories, especially if they have a personal element."

—Mary Matalin

....

"Public speakers don't work on the edge. They're not comedians. Since you don't work on the edge, there are two safe targets, you and people more powerful than you. Anything else, you run a risk."

—James Carville

"Practice your hand gestures in front of a mirror. You'd be surprised how many times a person telling a joke looks like one of those Irish dancers with the feet moving back and forth and the arms and hands glued to the side. Practice your jokes in front of your family."

—Jay Leno

....

"As a comedian I'm under pressure to be funny. If a comedian is not funny, he ends up doing a one-man show or becomes a performance artist where you speak for three hours and if you say anything that resembles a joke, the audience appreciates it. So if you're the president of Amalgamated Rubber Bands, no one expects you to be Milton Berle. Since there's no pressure to be funny, the first thing to do is just relax. And then pull out your cock."

—Gilbert Gottfried

....

"Here are some ways to connect with the audience. Come out shirtless, cover yourself up, and tell them you have complied with John Ashcroft's request. Alternately, bringing out a dead puppy that you then bring back to life is a surefire way to their hearts. Waving a gun will get the audience's attention, as well as security's and, sometime later, a court-ordered psychiatrist's."

—Bruce Vilanch

....

"First thing I do up front is to get the audience on my side. I take a breath and deliver the first joke calmly and in control. Let them know who you are with that first joke but never hand over your power to them."

—Stefanie Wilder

....

"There is no replacement for preparing and then listening to the other speakers to see if they say anything you want to play off of, but that requires some practice."

—George Schlatter

Crossfire's Paul Begala is a great speechwriter, a tremendous public speaker, and a man who advised Bill Clinton for eight-plus years—arguably one of the most charismatic speakers of our time. If there is anyone who can help you give a speech or address a group, Paul's the man.

PAUL BEGALA'S 6 TIPS ON PUBLIC SPEAKING

1. *Surprise 'em by doing the unexpected. It's all well and good for a liberal like me to make fun of Bush, but if I toss a barb at Clinton, they like it better.*

2. *Be self-deprecating. I use a line about how "being James Carville's partner is a little bit like being Dolly Parton's feet."*

3. *Stay within the Master Narrative. Go with what folks know. You wanna do a boob joke (see above), Dolly Parton's the one (she's still better known in my businessman audiences than Pamela Anderson). Quayle is dumb. Clinton is eatin' or cheatin'. Bush Junior is in over his head. Cheney is sickly. Now, none of those caricatures is fully accurate. Quayle is smarter than you think and Clinton hasn't been inside a McDonald's in years. But don't fight the Master Narrative.*

4. *Weave jokes into the body of the speech. The old high-school formula of starting with a joke then making three substantive points is useless. Make sure you have jokes, funny anecdotes, or humorous asides throughout the speech. Even if they seem to you to be somewhat off point. When I'm speaking about likely 2004 Democratic presidential candidates, I always mention Hillary, even though I know for a fact she*

ain't running. I mention her because I have a killer joke about her:

When Clinton appointed Hillary to run the health care reform, he caught grief from the right-wingers—who elected Hillary Clinton? So he told me to point out to the press that Dukakis had Hillary on his short list for secretary of education if he'd have won.

"Begala," he said, "you go out there and tell those reporters that if I'd never married Hillary I could appoint her to any job in the government and no one could say anything about it." To which I replied, "Mr. President, with all due respect, if you hadn't married Hillary you wouldn't be making any appointments in the government."

5. *Jokes are best when they help illustrate a point. The above joke is not only funny, it allows me to point out that, independent of her husband, Hillary was selected as one of the hundred best lawyers in America in 1990, and how she was on the corporate boards of Wal-Mart and TCBY long before her husband ran for president.*

6. *Singe, don't burn. Your goal is to make the audience like you. Don't do edgy stuff. You're not a trained professional and you're not going to be given the same freedom as a real comic. I always have to watch it when I do "Bush is dumb" jokes. I can't say half the things Jay Leno gets away with because: a) he's a pro;*

b) everyone knows it's only a joke with Jay; c) they know I truly don't like Bush and they think it's a cheap shot to go too far.

Here are some helpful hints on how to use jokes in public speaking (cut this out and put it in your wallet):

- *Open with a misdirection or a self-deprecating joke or a story about yourself.*
- *Say something topical.*
- *Make a joke acknowledging the format of the speech or connect to the company. ("It's an honor for me to speak to the insurance agents of America because of my close connection to your industry. I've totaled five cars.")*
- *Put two to four jokes up front.*
- *Stay serious during the key thrust of your speech, but don't be afraid to sprinkle jokes throughout.*
- *If you're not finishing inspirational, finish with a joke (leave 'em laughing).*

Here is an example of humor in a short five-minute speech by Senator John Kerry last March. The remarks were prepared by the senator, legendary speechwriter Bob Shrum, and members of the Kerry staff.

To set up the situation, one of the Boston newspapers had hired a genealogist to trace Kerry's roots. They revealed that contrary to what some believed in Massachusetts, he wasn't Irish (they had assumed it from his last name) and he had two Jewish-Austrian ancestors.

Throw in the fact that he was just coming off prostate surgery and it looked like the senator was going to miss, for the first time in years, the big St. Patrick's Day breakfast in Boston. The Boston press was in a minifrenzy about Kerry not being there and a critic or two suggested it was because he didn't want to face a predominantly Irish crowd after the story about his roots. Nothing could have been further from the truth. So the senator wanted to show up and use some humor to answer the critics.

HUMOR IN A SPEECH, LESSON 101

"Who said I didn't have the matza balls to be here today? Governor Romney, it's great to see you. My money's on Bulger. This may be a tough place but the truth is I had no hesitation coming here to a battle zone. After all, I may not be Irish, but I'm also not French. So let's get it straight: I'm Scottish, Scotch-Irish, English, Jewish, Austrian, Hungarian—I don't know why George Bush is going to the United Nations...I am the United Nations.

Let me give you a campaign update. As many of you know I recently had some work done on my shillelagh. As Teresa says, Boston isn't the only place that had a Big Dig. The difference is,

mine came in on time and on budget—because I
didn't have a Republican governor do it. I know a
number of you have wondered: Can a man be
elected president without a prostate? And I say
why not? We've had a number of Republican presidents elected without a heart.

And finally, I'd like to take just a moment to
reflect on St. Patrick's Day. Today we celebrate a
heritage that has enlivened and enriched the
heart and spirit of our country..."

Note: The local newspapers reported he stole
the show.

You have a lot more interesting and funny things to say
about yourself than you think. The key is to actually think.

**"You have to remember you are a collector, an
archaeologist of your own life. Telling something
about yourself makes it harmless. And your life
becomes a place to mine for anecdotes and
strew them in front of people you meet."**

—Carrie Fisher

In addition to the rules above, here are a few formula
jokes and bits that work well in any speech.

1. *The translation joke:* "*It's great to be here in Des
   Moines, which is Native American for nothing to do on
   a Saturday night.*"

2. *The "who isn't here" formula: this is a way to work in some topical references. "Martha Stewart couldn't be here tonight. She's under house arrest. Yasir Arafat couldn't be here. Wednesday is his night to go rock throwing. Woody Allen couldn't be here. His wife has homework." And then you transition to why you are thrilled to be there.*

3. *Giving rules for the evening: it's a formula that allows you to make fun of current events, people in the room, the format of the evening. You can do a takeoff on a great joke Billy Crystal did at the Oscars a few years ago in which he talked about the evacuation order in the room in the event of an earthquake. When you do it, mention the CEO on down to the copy-room boy and then end with the vice president.*

Reactive Humor

Before any speech I tell my clients to be prepared for the unexpected with an ad-lib.

You should think through all the possible minor things that could go wrong and plan on what to say: if a cell phone rings, how to handle a heckler, what happens if the lights go out or the microphone goes dead.

One day in the middle of Jay's monologue, a cell phone rang in the audience. Jay didn't get angry, he didn't have the person evicted; that's not his style. Instead he walked into the audience and right there on national television he said, "Here, let me talk to your friend." He answered the woman's phone saying, "This is Jay Leno. I'm in the middle of my monologue right now, so is there a message I can take?"

As a nonpro, you won't have the comedy chops to handle a ringing cell phone the way Jay did. But you can embarrass the rude person into silence or compliance with one of these.

5 Things to Say If a Cell Phone Rings When You're Speaking

1. *"If that's for me, tell them I'm busy, I'm giving a speech."*

2. *"Ask her what she's wearing."*

3. *"Tell them the check is in the mail."*

4. *"If that's Phil Spector, just hang up."*

5. *"If that's my wife, tell her I'm with you."*

What happens if your worst nightmare comes true, if someone starts acting rude, heckling, talking loud to his neighbor during your speech, walking in late or walking out early? The key is to do exactly what a comic does at a nightclub. With a smile and an arrow, make that person the collective target of the audience.

Let's take the example of someone talking loud while you're giving your speech. Here are some things you can say.

1. *"Now I know why lions eat their young."* (*a favorite of Rodney Dangerfield*)

2. *"I guess the medication is wearing off. Someone notify his caretaker."*

3. *"Could you speak a little louder? We all missed the part about the Viagra not working."*

• •

FREE OPENING STORY FOR YOUR SPEECH, COURTESY OF GEORGE SCHLATTER

One day the emperor was feeding the Christians to the lions. Finally the last Christian, whose name was Michael, was brought out. The lion rushed up to him and was about to pounce when Michael said, "Come over here." The lion stopped dead in his tracks. He tiptoed up to Michael, and Michael whispered in the lion's ear. Next thing you know, the lion turned pale, ran off into the corner, and hid. He refused to come out. The emperor was beside himself. He asked Michael, "What did you say to the lion?" Michael wouldn't answer. The emperor then said, "Tell me what you said to make the lion act like that and I'll set you free." Michael didn't say a word. Finally the emperor said, "If you tell me what you whispered to the lion that made him panic like that, I'll set all your countrymen free." Michael walked up to the emperor and said, "I told the lion that after dinner, he was expected to say a few words."

ANOTHER STORY GOOD AT A FUND-RAISING EVENT

This one is good for any fund-raising event at which there is a well-known individual who collects the money. For this story, I'll use Allied Jewish Appeal. You can use any big fund-raising organization.

"About two weeks ago the Silbermintzes were flying on vacation. All of a sudden the plane developed engine trouble, the radio went out, and the pilot got on the intercom. He said that he was going to have to make an emergency landing, he could see a deserted island in the distance, they would all be safe but that no one would ever find them. As the plane was landing Mrs. Silbermintz asked her hus-

band, "Did you make out our will?" Mr. Silbermintz
said he had. A minute later she asked, "Did you tell
the kids we love them?" He told her he had done
so. She then asked if he had made the $10,000
pledge to Allied Jewish Appeal. He said it was the
last thing he did before getting on the flight. She
then asked, "Did you send them the check?" He said
he hadn't sent it. Mrs. Silbermintz sat back completely relaxed. "Don't worry, they'll find us."

SOME MORE TIPS FROM THE PROS
ON PUBLIC SPEAKING

A warning from Buz Kohan, the winner of thirteen
Emmys and a universally beloved funny and nice guy,
who says that the most important thing in giving a
speech is to know your audience:

> "One time my wife was giving a speech to a ban-
> quet and she did a few jokes about why patients
> hate doctors. It was a banquet of cardiologists."
> —Buz Kohan

KEY:

> "Know exactly who your audience is. If your boss
> is there and he's a born-again, keep your jokes
> clean. If it's all men and they know about

sports, you can make jokes about sports. If it's half men and half women, tailor your jokes accordingly. Don't exclude people in the audience, be inclusive."

—Jay Leno

....

"Know your audience . . . and get a laugh early. In the first sixty seconds you must get a laugh to set a tone and let your audience know they are in for a pleasant ride."

—Arsenio Hall

....

"Get to know someone in the group you're going to be addressing and have them give you some inside information on a couple of people they know will be there and, if possible, a few details about the competition. When you drop in those references, you'll connect on their level, which makes it easier for them to laugh with you."

—Paul Harris

"Keep a list of great jokes and things people have said that make you laugh. Use them in your speech."

—George Schlatter

....

"Remember, if you're an after-dinner speaker don't live on the edge. You're not Howard Stern."

—James Carville

....

"The advice I always give to public speakers is to 'know your audience.' I wish I dreamt it up myself, but it's something Billy Crystal has told the Oscar writers for many years. Whenever one of us would pitch a scathingly pointed joke about an Oscar nominee, we'd all laugh and assume Billy would use it. Then, we'd be shocked when he said no. 'Know your audience, fellas. It's the Oscars, not the Friar's club. It's not a roast. These people have been nominated for an important award and it's not time to make fun of them.' Certain targets are exempt from this rule, Jack Nicholson, for example, because he's such a bigger-than-life character who is very self-deprecating and well liked. The audience knows he's in on the joke. However, you can't go out on Oscar night and start making fun of Julianne Moore without coming off as mean-spirited. Olympic gold-medalist Scott Hamilton told me a great story about another athlete who was being honored at a dinner in the midwest. When he got up to accept, he used every dirty word and racial slur in the book, thinking he was being funny. It got so bad, the local cops hustled him off the stage. The next day, the town demanded an apology. The sports star was quoted in the local paper saying, 'I guess I misread the room.' Bottom line, you know your audience."

—Dave Boone

2. How to Be Funny at Work

"From the sound of it, offices must be funny because every single person comes up to me and says, 'Come to my office, you can get a lot of material there.' I then have to explain to them that Hank coming in half an hour late isn't the type of humor I do."

—Gilbert Gottfried

What happens at your office isn't going to work for Gilbert—but it can work for you. There are any number of ways and situations where you can be funny on the job.

Proactive Situations

GIVING A PEP TALK TO YOUR STAFF (BOSS TO EMPLOYEES)

As always, let's start with what doesn't work. If you want to make sure that a talk to your staff does not inspire anyone, use a lot of charts, graphs, and words like *synergy, impacting,* and *retrenchment.* What you want to do is get their attention and have them bond as a team. So at the beginning of your talk and sprinkled throughout, say things to keep them on edge and make them laugh.

1. *Start out by talking about what your competition is doing at their sales meeting and make fun of them by way of comparison: "Right now the boss of XYZ is telling his staff to give 110 percent. It's math like that, that got American Airlines in trouble. They've got horrible conditions over there. Their office is so cold, people are standing next to Hillary Clinton for warmth."*

2. *Use self-deprecation: "Why am I up here today talking to you when we all know you are the reason for the success of this company? It's because of three factors. My hard work, my determination, and the fact that I married the owner's daughter."*

    At a campaign rally (the political equivalent of a pep talk) last fall for Ballot Proposition 49, Arnold Schwarzenegger knew that he was going to be asked if this was a first step toward running for governor. He said that he couldn't even think about running for governor because the forms were so complicated. And besides, if he listed "actor" as his occupation on the form, they could charge him with perjury.

3. *Say the opposite of what you mean: "I think we need to work on a few things. As a company, we need to take more time playing solitaire on the computer. We need to get our company softball team back in first place. We need to spend more time on the Internet e-mailing friends. And it is then and only then that we should spend time making this company more productive so we can have bigger bonuses."*

GIVING A PRESENTATION (EMPLOYEE TO BIGWIGS)

In this situation, unless you're giving a speech to a large group, I recommend using humor in three specific places:

- to introduce yourself and your topic.
- to break up sections of your presentation or to make a key point.
- during the Q & A (this is really reactive humor off their key words).

"The most difficult but most effective humor is to throw in impromptu funny asides as you are answering questions."

—Mary Matalin

Here's a good opening: "For those of you who don't know me really well, I'm Bob Smith and I've been told that in any presentation like this, it's best to tell the truth. [pause] I'm a winner of the Congressional Medal of Honor, I received the 1996 Academy Award for best actor, I had a sixteen hundred on my college boards, and I'm a multi-millionaire. And for fun, my hobby is talking about [fill in topic of talk].

ASKING FOR A RAISE

This is a tricky one, as most people are too nervous when asking for more money to do anything but beg. But what better way to take the tension off than by adding a little humor. I suggest this. After you make the formal pitch, you can try ending it with an old classic. "The real question is, do I deserve it? Well, I have flat feet, high cholesterol, and ungrateful kids, and I don't deserve them. On the other hand, I think I deserve a raise. Plus it will help me deal with the flat feet, high cholesterol, and ungrateful kids."

THE OFFICE CHRISTMAS PARTY

Anything you say can and will be used against you. Do not get drunk, make sex jokes, or grope anyone. Instead, make yourself the center of the circle by being the storyteller. Stories about past family holidays from hell, former employees who were hated and have departed, and jokes about the food and drink at other nonoffice parties are always good. Try a few of these:

1. *"I have nothing bad to say about Abe. Or his toupee."*

2. *"The food at the last party was really bad. Afterwards, I tested positive for Crisco."*

3. *"They say this is like family here but it's not true. If it were like my family, three of you would be with parole officers."*

As always, I turn to Eddie Driscoll for advice on what not to do at an office party. He said, "It's always a good idea to open up the conversation by making fun of recently deceased relatives. Then after a couple of drinks you can really let loose."

Reactive Situations

DEALING WITH HARASSMENT

There's a step in between punching someone who has been harassing you and filing an EEOC complaint. It's called humor. Only you can decide on the level of humor/anger you want to use, but if you can make the harasser's peers laugh at him, he may, just may, shut up.

> HARASSER: If I said you had a beautiful body, would you hold it against me?

> YOU AT LEVEL 1 RESPONSE: I would but I can't handle the pressure of being with such a quick and original mind.

> YOU AT LEVEL 2 RESPONSE: It's amazing. You're not working but your Viagra is.

> YOU AT DEFCOM 3: And make the UPS guys jealous? They tell me you are hot.

RUINING A RIVAL'S PRESENTATION

Okay, maybe this isn't nice but there may be an all-time prick in the office who deserves it. The key is to react off of words in his presentation or to use the all-important moment when he or she says, "Any questions?"

At that point you turn the focus of the meeting off of him and back to you with something along these lines (these are current for summer 2003; update for something topical from that week for you).

> RIVAL: Any questions?
> YOU: Yes, who do you think will win *American Idol*?
> YOU: Do you think the Clintons will stay together?
> YOU: Yes, do you think Ben Affleck wears a toupee?

. . . .

SOME QUICK ADVICE FOR BEING FUNNY IN YOUR PROFESSION

How to be funny...
If you're a politician:

Rule number one, make fun of yourself. I love something like this: "I was an Eagle Scout, I started my own business, built my company up from scratch, I fought in Desert Storm, came back, and now I'm running to be your congressman. And right now you're all thinking, Where did the boy go wrong?"

Here are some other classics:

"I will always be remembered as the man who accompanied Jackie Kennedy to Paris."

—John F. Kennedy

. . . .

"I have a face for radio."

—Paul Simon

. . . .

"I'm from Massachusetts, which is an old Native American word for 'land of many Kennedys.' "

—Senator John Kerry

. . . .

If you're a pro athlete:

Look at Charles Barkley and Terry Bradshaw, two very funny athletes. Charles makes fun of others, Terry makes fun of himself. Either way, it's effective. Terry has some great lines. Here are some he gave while speaking at a golf luncheon.

"Do you know the single hardest part about golf for me? Adding up the score. I had a ninety-six this morning. The last time I got a ninety-six was on my SAT's.

"You know my handicap—I'm bald, dumb, and have three ex-wives."

"Mom learned how to play golf. They've got a new course in state prison."

If you're a lawyer:

Use the politician joke above, substituting *lawyer*.

If you're a funny waitress:

As a waitress, you want to be funny and get some sympathy with light sarcasm. Funny waitresses get nice tips. Topless waitresses get even bigger tips but that's for my next book. So for your basic nontopless waitress, try something like this. "Before I take your order, I want you to know I'm really a member of the royal family. This is one of those princess and the pauper situations, and I just waitress as a hobby."

3. *How Humor Can Help Handle an Awkward or Tense Situation*

How many times have you been in a situation where someone says something completely inappropriate? Sometimes it's the socially clueless person who speaks of rope in the house of the condemned (asking someone about his wife two weeks after a divorce); it might be a comment made out of ignorance about race or religion (hello, Trent Lott!); or it can be someone making a wildly idiotic statement about a horrible tragedy in the news way too soon before it's funny (note—as Johnny Carson once said, it's still too soon to tell Lincoln jokes).

And no matter how strange the situation, no matter how tense, the person who *can* tell a joke can help.

> "Using humor to defuse a tense situation is a common occurrence at the White House because there are nothing but tense situations and there are a lot of funny, clever people here. The president and vice president have wicked senses of humor. They are both keen observers of the human condition, which is the source of all the great jokes."
>
> —Mary Matalin

. . . .

> "A few years back I created a peaceful community day where at-risk youth could meet, talk to, and socialize with LAPD officers. I hadn't expected to do stand-up that day but it turned out to be one of my most important and spontaneous monologues. As you can imagine, at some point during that long, hot day, tempers flared during a heated conversation on the topic of police brutality. Humor became the hero and equalizer in the situation. Making a group laugh can momen-

tarily ease tension. It's simply very hard to focus
on your hate when you are laughing. A satirical
rant about myself running from cops in Cleve-
land when I was a teenager did the trick."
—Arsenio Hall

If Mary and Arsenio can find humor in the most tense
situations imaginable, you can find it and use it too.

I find the best way to handle an awkward social comment—assuming you don't want to punch someone
out—is to be the bigger person and ease the awkward-
ness or change the subject with a joke. These are all reactive situations, as you are trying to ease the tension after
someone has said or done something stupid.

A new biography about Sandy Koufax by Jane Leavey
discusses how difficult it was for him as one of the few
Jewish players in the majors. (And of course there are so
many now.) The author cited two examples of him using
jokes to lighten an awkward situation. The first involved
a time the team had a party at Duke Snider's house. There
was a pig roast in the backyard, and Snider's wife was
concerned about what Sandy would eat. He pointed to
the pig and said, "I'll have some of that turkey."

Another time Koufax was on a bus going through
Miami when one of the Dodger coaches yelled out, "You
can give this damn town back to the Jews." Koufax said,
"Billy, we already own it."

Both approaches worked. One was a kind, funny way of easing tension, the other used the hidden truth to make a point.

Now here's an example of a celebrity handling an awkward situation incredibly wrong. In October 2002, Ryan Adams was singing in concert and one of the fans yelled out, "Sing 'Summer of 69.' " Which of course is by Bryan Adams. Ryan Adams could have done any number of funny things to endear himself to the world. He could have:

- *begun singing "Summer of 69," stopped after eight notes, and said, "Wait a second, I'm not Bryan Adams, I'm Ryan Adams."*
- *said, "His concert is next week but I can get you tickets."*
- *said, "I can't sing 'Summer of 69' although I'm a big fan of the number."*

He could have done just about anything except what he did, which was to stop his concert, demand the fan leave, have him escorted out, and personally hand him $30. Fortunately his manager realized what an asshole Ryan Adams was and got the fan back in. Remember, always use humor to be bigger than everyone else, not smaller.

Now, what happens when you do something stupid and embarrassing—rip your pants, wear the wrong clothes, show up on the wrong day to a dinner party? Or in my case, do all three? I always recommend going right at it with any of these.

SITUATION: You rip your pants/wear wildly inappropriate clothes.
YOUR COMMENT: "Anything I can do to help the troubled textile industry by wearing cheaply made clothes no one else will wear, hey, it makes me proud to be an American."

SITUATION: You show up on the wrong date for an event.
YOUR COMMENT: "This is kind of a test run— no, no need to feed me tonight, I'm just seeing how quick you could act if this were a real emergency."

SITUATION: You pass gas.
YOUR COMMENT: "I'm going to buy a dog just so I can have somebody to blame."

4. How to Be Funny in School

I think I developed my sense of humor as protection in school. I was one of five Jewish kids in a class of 550 people, not a very good athlete and not one of the "tough guys." In that situation you can allow yourself to be ridiculed and beaten to a pulp...or you can be the class crack-up, the funny guy, the person who can always make people laugh.

In addition to enabling you to live long enough to graduate, being funny has some real advantages in school.

- *It helps you impress teachers. Teachers love the kid with the sense of humor as long as you know when to use it. I would always use it during a discussion of current events—good preparation for later becoming a monologue writer; I would use it after a stupid announcement over the loudspeaker; and I would use it as the opening of an essay.*
- *It helps you get dates. Women love someone who can make them laugh.*
- *It can help you rise to become the almost alpha male or head Heather. My advice—in the jungle of high school, use your alpha wit to attack the betas in the herd; in other words, point out the weak wildebeest before the jackals turn on you. If I had been in high school with Al Gore, I would have been all over his case from day one.*
- *It makes you king of the lunchroom. One of the first times I realized I was funny and could tell a story was in the lunchroom. It's the perfect place to gather around and aim your humor at a familiar shared target—teachers and school officials.*
- *It helps you deal with bullies. Before I give you some tips on how being funny can help you handle a bully,*

let me tell you how not to handle a bully. It can be found in one of these pamphlets going around now called "How to Protect Your Child from a Bully" and it emphasizes to parents that their child is a victim and that bullies pick on the small and weak and that the best thing to do is have your child tell the bully that he will tell the bully's parents. Get a clue, people—bullies generally come from dysfunctional families. White trash mom may be proud that her kid is a budding Gestapo agent or SS guard. I'm sure that dinner conversation in that house is "Hey Vern, Marvin's beating up the Jew boy, give him some more Tater Tots."

The way to handle a bully is not to be small but to be big and strong on a different field of battle. You want to dazzle the bully with your quick wit and move him to turf familiar to you but unfamiliar to him. You want to dazzle with your way with words. Cut this out and put it on the refrigerator.

Here are 3 things to say to the bully...
and remember, keep talking a mile a minute.

Step 1—"Look, I don't want any trouble. For three reasons. One, I'm a bleeder. Two, because when Billy said you were a punk, I told Billy that if his sister had as many pricks sticking out of her as she has stuck into her, she'd

*be a porcupine, and three, I can be a giant help because
I've got a mouth that won't quit. You want to put somebody down, I'm your DH, designated humor guy."*

*Step 2—"So here's the plan. You tell me who you want to
insult, I'll help. For example, the cafeteria ladies. I
thought there was a rule against mustaches in school.
And the guys in the chess club. I think they're on
steroids."*

*Step 3—"But you got to promise you won't tell my parents
I'm helping you. They'll tell your parents and then I'll
get in trouble for being your assistant."*

ANOTHER EXAMPLE: You're in your freshman
year of high school and the captain of the football
team is trying to prove how tough he is by knocking over your books in the hall and then asking if
you plan to do anything about it.

Best thing to do is talk fast and key off his word *plan.*
Tell him you have no plans to fight because you're
already scheduled to fight the winner of the fight between
(name two nerds) and that's for the WBA title—Wimp
Boxing Association. But if he's patient and wants to
move down a weight class, tell him you'll see if you can
pencil him in for next October.

And if that doesn't work, flee.

GARRY SHANDLING ON HOW BEING FUNNY CAN HELP YOU AVOID CONFLICTS

"I've always used humor as a defense mechanism to both smooth over conflict and avoid confrontation and fights. One time, five years ago, Oscar de la Hoya got really mad at me. It was two minutes into round three. This is when I was boxing professionally. I had repeatedly hit him with low blows and I could tell he was going to kill me. In a clinch I said to him, 'You know, I used to be a swimsuit model in the "I can't believe it's a guy" catalog.' He started laughing and we patched things up right there. The fight was declared a draw."

—Garry Shandling

5. *How to Be Funny on the Phone*

Proactive Humor

HAVE A FUNNY MESSAGE ON YOUR ANSWERING MACHINE

First of all, have a funny phone message. The best in America are by my friend Bruce Vilanch. He changes them every day and people call him up just to hear what he has to say. If you don't have time to change it every day, change it once a week, with a reference to something topical. Here was my message back in October 2002: "Hi, this is Jon. I'm not in right now. Randy Moss and I are out knocking down meter maids with a Lexus. If you want to join us, leave a message."

LEAVING A FUNNY MESSAGE FOR SOMEONE ON HIS PHONE

This is your chance to leave a quick joke. Since the person you called won't be expecting it when he retrieves his messages, it automatically has the key ingredient of surprise.

Here are a few samples you can try:

- *"Hey, this is Jon. I had a dream that we won the lottery with these three numbers. Play them no matter what. Twenty-three, thirty-six..." (hang up phone)*
- *"Here's your quote of the day from the great Christina Aguilera. 'Some people aspire to greatness, some people have greatness thrust upon them, some have greatness thrust into them.' "*
- *(if after noon) "Look, if you call me before noon I can get us two dates with some flight attendants."*
- *"You know what I found out today? Folgers is not the best part of waking up."*
- *"If the police call, I was with you all morning."*

Reactive Humor

ENDING A PHONE CONVERSATION

I like ending a conversation by summing it up with a twist. One day a friend called me and for thirty minutes he was asking for advice on how to take care of his ill father, telling me about problems with his mom, asking how to handle his real estate and how to manage a job switch. Then at one point as we were finishing up he recommended a book for me to read. I said, "So let me get this straight. I straighten out your dysfunctional family, handle your parents, change your life, give you investment tips that will make you $200,000, and in return I get a book review? Sounds fair to me."

TORTURING TELEMARKETERS

This is one of those rare situations where you are not trying to make someone else laugh, you are doing this just for your own amusement. The minute the telemarketer calls and asks for you, just tell him/her the story of your sex change operation. Every single detail. Ask the telemarketer if he/she has ever thought about getting in touch with the woman or man within.

LISTENING TO THE PERSON ON THE OTHER END OF THE LINE

As always, key in on a word he uses. The best way to give good phone is to listen to what the other person is saying and react to a word he uses. Or take your life and share the weirdness. No matter how strange a day your friend on the phone had, yours was stranger.

6. *How to Write Funny E-Mails*

Being funny in an e-mail does not mean forwarding a joke to seventy-five people. It may be funny—but it doesn't mean *you* are funny. Being funny in an e-mail also does not mean using :). It does mean being original when you send someone a message.

This is a thank-you I got from Rita Rudner for a gift we sent her for her new baby.

> Jon—
> Thank you so much for the great presents. Here's a picture as she's about to be weighed and measured for the four-month entry on her growth chart cube. She weighs about seventy pounds and is three feet tall. Is that wrong?
>> Rita

Or in this day and age of e-mail gossip, you can use a funny e-mail to stop a rumor. A number of people in our local youth baseball league started e-mailing each other with the rumor I had been taken to the hospital with a heart attack the day before I was supposed to run our sign-ups. This is how I handled it.

Everyone—

Several people have called very concerned about
a rumor I had a heart attack. Although I would
fake just about anything to get out of sign-ups, it
is not true. So for those who called to see if they
could help, thanks!

For those who called out of wishful thinking,
sorry!

And for those who were more concerned about
sign-ups, that's the true spirit and if I do have a
heart attack tonight, the forms are in the front
corner of my garage.

See you Saturday,

Jon

Proactive Humor

The best way to send a funny e-mail is to take advantage
of the fact that people can't see you. At the same time,
since they can't see your face, they can't tell when you
are being sarcastic. So stay away from the sarcasm and
instead, use the lack of direct sensory input to enable
you to paint a fake picture of where you are and what
you're doing.

Jim—

Sorry about the delay in getting back to you but
the police are just wrapping up. God, it takes so

long for them to draw one of those chalk body outlines.

Anyway...

Reactive Humor

Unfortunately, people often use e-mail to vent at a distance when they don't have the balls to say something to your face. I think the best way to react to that is by correcting their grammar and giving them notes, suggestions, and comments, then giving them a grade on their e-mail and telling them you are happy to help whenever they need some guidance on writing.

ENDING ANNOYING INSTANT MESSAGING

Last summer *Time* magazine featured an article on instant messaging. In the article, a consultant was plugging this new program connected to IM, which enables a person to gracefully end the conversation by somehow "waving good-bye" followed by a countdown.

How fucking rude. You're just giving someone a countdown and then cutting him off. Okay, I'm filing for divorce in three days: 3, 2, 1, bye! How about giving them a joke instead?

- *"Look I have to go, the battery on the Rampant Rabbit is running down."*

- *"I'd love to keep IMing but I'm throwing you overboard right now for someone paying me."*
- *"Got to go, bad burrito for lunch."*
- *"Oh my God, someone is willing to sell me naked pictures over the Internet. I bet I'm the only one. Got to go."*
- *"I don't want to creep you out but I'm getting an instant message right now from Princess Margaret. I'll fill you in later."*

7. How to Be Funny in a Job Interview

This is similar to using humor when asking for a raise. There's an advantage to being funny in the interview because it sets you apart from the other applicants and it sets you apart from being some geeky Dilbert in a cubicle. But again, know your audience.

Proactive Humor

The most important thing you can do is to take charge of the interview and deliver the message you want about yourself. Step 1 is to establish a bond and break the ice with the interviewer by getting him or her on your side with some light conversation about the weather, a local major sports event, something common that you are both aware of. For example, if I were interviewing for a job after the Yankees lost to the Angels, I'd make small talk about the game, the Yankees, and then comment,

"Well, at least Steinbrenner's not the type to overreact."

You get the laugh and then begin your serious spiel about who you are.

I'd also be proactive in explaining why you left your last job. You might want to say something about the fact that although United Airlines is a wonderful company, your dad always told you never to work at a place where you can buy the company stock at the 99¢ store.

Reactive Humor

In a job interview, you know you will be asked one of the following three questions, so in advance, prepare a funny response, deliver the joke when asked the antici-pated questions, and then when the interviewer is help-less with laughter, finish him off with your real answer, the serious knockout punch.

Let's say you're applying for an entry-level job as a receptionist.

QUESTION 1: What are your salary requirements?
YOU: Between us, Bill Gates and I want to make $3,000,045,000 next year.

QUESTION 2: Why do you want to work here?
YOU: I understand you have great rest rooms. In addition, ... (serious response)

155

QUESTION 3: What special qualities will you bring to the job?

YOU: You mean besides my ninety-five words per minute typing, my cheerful, chipper phone voice, the fact I can play a great third base for the company softball team, and my willingness to work a hundred hours a week?... Other than that, I don't bring much.

8. Special Social Functions

There are social situations during which we are called upon to say something meaningful.

THE ROAST

The roast is a common device used by charities, at bachelor parties, and at retirement dinners to provide entertainment and some humor.

Think of Jeffrey Ross's 5 Rules of Insult Humor, except it's more formal. Instead of sitting around and busting chops among friends, you are going to be doing it in front of an audience.

I suggest using a standard format that a lot of the pros use.

1. *Start by talking about why you were chosen to speak. Something self-deprecating is good here to let them know you are able to make fun of yourself.*

2. *Acknowledge who else is speaking. This is a way to get in a joke or two about the other people speaking that night.*

3. *Make mention of who isn't there. You can do this by talking about loved ones who didn't bother to make it or about celebrities. For example, you can mention that Calista Flockhart was going to be there but she heard they were serving food.*

   Here's a good example taken from Billy Crystal's roast of Rob Reiner on Comedy Central:

   "And where is your good friend Al Gore? He can spend two days raising illegal money from Buddhist nuns but he won't spend an hour with you. Rob is telling everyone he's going to get Al Gore elected president. Great, something else they can blame on the Jews. Where's Joe Lieberman? I know, it's a Friday night and he can't come out. If he really liked you, he would have walked.

   "George W. Bush isn't here. Why not? If anyone in the world can appreciate someone who coasted through life on his father's name it's George W. Bush."

4. *Explain why you're there. "I am here for one very important reason. My TV set is broken."*

5. *Describe your relationship to the roastee. This is good for a story or some jokes.*

6. *And then go to six to eight jokes about the roastee.*
   - *You can work on the physical—"She's so old her vagina has mice." (a Jeffrey Ross joke)*
   - *The mental—"He graduated college with a blood alcohol higher than his GPA."*
   - *His marriages—"They always say fifth time is the charm."*
   - *His failures—"Admittedly there have been business problems. His new book on financial advice starts and ends with a chapter eleven."*
   - *His looks—"He's so ugly hookers stand him up."*

And you can do all of this because at the end, you're going to say what a great person the roastee is.

"We always roast the ones we love."

—Jeffrey Ross

THE WEDDING TOAST

Think back. What do you remember most about any wedding toast? Do you remember the long toast where the best man drunkenly tries to recount some ancient, boring story about the couple and how much they love each other, or do you remember the funny toast that got everyone at the reception laughing? Short of reminding the assembled masses that 50 percent of all marriages end in divorce and that statistically, there is a 45 percent chance one of the partners will be unfaithful within three years, here are some tips:

1. *Reference how long they've been together if it's a long engagement.*
    "When they started dating, Iraq was called Mesopotamia."
    "When they started dating, Joan Collins was young."
    "When they started dating, Lincoln supported the NRA."

Or reference how short their relationship is: "They've known each other two months. I've known cable repairmen longer than that."

2. *Mention the cost of the reception by saying the opposite. If it's extravagant, talk about how cheap the bride's dad is: "The least he could have done is opened up the wallet. It's his only daughter and he's only got three bands and a rented helicopter. Come on, filet? What's wrong with a couple Taco Bell chalupas and a six-pack of Bud?"*

3. *Most important, make fun of the groom, make fun of yourself, make fun of the event ("It's so hot Joe had two reasons to sweat"). Just never make fun of the bride.*

ADDED HINT: You can always read fake telegrams from celebrities:

"Tom Green reminds everyone to have a ball."

"The Pope says don't do anything he wouldn't do."

Saddam Hussein—"I'd love to be there but I'm spending this weekend getting bombed."

Billy Bob Thornton—"Remember, love goes but tattoos are forever."

Dick Cheney—"Love makes my heart go pitter-patter. So does a defibrillator."

Eddie Driscoll's 5 Tips for What Not to Do While Giving a Wedding Toast

1. *Remind everyone you nailed the bride's sister.*

2. *Remind the groom that you once nailed the bride.*

3. *Spend a lot of time trying to find a word for your tribute poem that rhymes with "high hard one."*

4. *End by jumping into the cake.*

5. *Speak for more than two hours.*

BREAKING UP/AFTER THE DIVORCE

First a warning: Do not be funny while actually breaking up or leaving someone. That will allow the jury to acquit your ex-beloved on a defense of justifiable homicide. These are tips on how to let everyone else know after the breakup that 1) you are no longer attached and 2) you don't care.

> Q: Hey, Joe, how's Cindy?
> YOU: According to her new boyfriend, fine. It was the usual irreconcilable differences. Especially after she boiled the rabbit.

> Q: So, Cindy, where's Joe?
> YOU: It's over between us, but fortunately, I didn't catch anything from him.

> Q: I can't believe it, you and Susie have split up after twenty years.
> YOU: Split up is the wrong word. Getting paroled is more accurate.

MEETING THE GIRLFRIEND'S PARENTS/MEETING YOUR BOYFRIEND'S PARENTS

There is only one rule about kidding with your new love's parents: Never ever ever kid about sex.

Don't mention it. Not even if you're having a beer with her dad and a Victoria's Secret commercial comes on TV. Because the minute you mention sex, the parents will think of you as a pervert (her parents) or slut (his parents).

Stick with making fun of your extended family, go with the embarrassing story from your job, or poke fun at something in current events. Then get the hell out of Dodge.

THE EULOGY

This is not a roast. Even if it's a cremation, let the undertaker do the roasting. Your job is to tell funny stories about your relationship with the deceased in which he is wise and kind and you are the "victim."

"I first met Jim back in 1961. Back then things were different. We were in college and I had hair."

"I always try out my eulogy material by dropping by other funerals on open casket night."

—Eddie Driscoll

THE BAR MITZVAH

They're paying good money, so this audience wants to see some entertainment. What you want to do, given the fact you are only thirteen, is to suck up to them by talking about what the day means to you and use a misdirection joke: "Today there was a big change in my life. And that was just my voice."

You can also make fun of a target—your parents and their nerves or your siblings. In the end, you can always use a top-ten list, an easy format by which you can get everyone involved. Here are five starter jokes for your own list.

5 Reasons I'm Glad I'm Jewish

5. *"Twelve days of Christmas, one day of gifts; eight days of Hanukkah, eight days of gifts."*

4. *"In the event I trip and fall at the reception, there are plenty of doctors . . . and lawyers."*

3. *"There's no better way to end the evening than with a Rabbi Eliezer story."*

2. *"Easter eggs taste like crap."*

1. *"Elvis was reportedly Jewish. Hey, an overweight guy with gold chains and a leisure suit in Las Vegas. It's possible."*

THE CHARITY EVENT
Here are three never-fail tips.

1. *Point out that this is a worthwhile cause by pointing out so many nonworthwhile causes: "You chose to give*

*money here to the Diabetes Fund, which is better use of
your money than donating to the Foundation to Keep
Anna Nicole Smith's Next Husband on Life Support."*

2. *Be self-deprecating.*

3. *Make a light comment poking fun at the host of the
event; they always like someone to point out what a
fanatic they are at collecting money.*

9. Being Funny in That Special Moment

Until you are ready, here are some "gimmes," examples
to use in situations that can happen on any given day to
any of us. These are all reactive.

TALKING TO THE ANNOYING PARENT OF A CHILD
Is there anything more annoying than parents who can't
stop bragging about their child or filling you in on the
boring minutiae of their lives? If you live in a town like
Agoura Hills, every baby-booming soccer mom and every
overachieving dad will tell you they are the busiest parents, that their day is the most hectic, and that their
child is the next Brandi Chastain or Peyton Manning.

Whatever you do, do not play "Can you top this?"
That will then cause them to try and top you to
prove that they are the most and the best. Instead, use

Carrie Fisher's advice and play "Can you bottom this?"

Make fun of your child and your marriage in such a way that they stop talking about their own wonderchild as they stare at you in amazement; not only will this shut them up, hopefully, they will see what an idiot they sound like.

> ANNOYING PARENT: And Johnnie's teacher
> says he is a straight-A student.
> YOU: The only way my kid will come home with
> an A is if she commits adultery.
> ANNOYING PARENT CONTINUES: He has a 4.0
> average and is accepted to Yale.
> YOU: Isn't that where Son of Sam went to school?
> AND FINALLY, THE CONVERSATION ENDER:
> Talking about your little Cindy is fascinating.
> Next time, could we talk about your pets? I bet
> your dog is the Lassie of the neighborhood.

WHEN YOU BREAK WIND

"One great place to use humor to defuse a situation—when someone cuts the cheese in an elevator. A place where humor can't help—when they've just found a Swiss Army knife in your hand luggage at LaGuardia."

—Bruce Vilanch

If you're caught cutting the cheese, you're caught. I always say the best thing to do is go right at it.

- *"Clear out the coal mine, the canary died."*
- *"I'm going to buy a dog just so next time I can blame it on him."*
- *"Man, the food is good here."*
- *"Smells like teen spirit."*

WHEN YOU FORGET SOMEONE'S NAME/SENIOR MOMENT

Once again, the best way to handle this embarrassing social situation is to go right at it. Mention all the other things you've forgotten in a quick round of "I can bottom this": "Look, forgetting your name is bad enough. I forgot the pill three times and we ended up with Frank Jr., Cindy, and Brittany," or, "This is the second most embarrassing time I blanked on someone's name. But if the Pope can forgive me, so can you."

WHEN YOU ARE HAVING SEX FOR THE FIRST TIME WITH SOMEONE

Being able to joke around during this moment can set the tone for the whole relationship, plus for a guy, it has the added advantage of lowering expectations.

Try something like this: "Look, this is the first time we're together. And to be honest, I'm nervous. I haven't been with anyone since the alien abduction."

Or: "I wish we could be in Canada because under the exchange rate, my waist is only forty inches."

> **"Being funny on a date, yes. It's the getting laid part that never worked for me. Although whenever I've had sex, the girl is always laughing at the end."**
> **—Gilbert Gottfried**

CAVEAT: In your kidding, make sure to follow Carrie Fisher's advice: Never say anything weirdly funny that makes them want to stop having sex with you.

IMPOTENCY
Again, this happens to everyone. Well, not everyone. Dwell on that thought for a while, pasta penis. Again, I recommend going right at it, with imagery: "Look, it's not me, it's you. Your job is to talk about rockets blasting off, a train entering a tunnel, waterfalls. I need help."

BEING TOLD YOU HAVE SIX MONTHS TO LIVE
I think Warren Zevon handled this about as good as anyone ever has. He had some great songs but nothing he wrote was as classic as this, when he revealed to the world he was dying: "I'm OK with it, but it'll be a drag if I don't make it until the next James Bond movie comes out."

EXPLAINING YOUR BOTOX INJECTION/PLASTIC SURGERY/NEW BREASTS

I suggest self-deprecation with a dead-pan expression (if the Botox will allow it): "You may have noticed something different about me. Let me use a euphemism. I had the builders in to do some work down on the 'house.' We reinforced the sagging bottom, filled in some chipped paint, and expanded the upstairs... on ... my ... house."

10. Intro to Comebacks 101

But of all the things people ask me about, they most often want to know how to handle it when someone says something mean.

First of all, to prepare, you need to watch the great African-American comics at a comedy club. Then reread "Playing the Dozens" at the end of Chapter Three. Once that is done, and before we work on your withering comeback, which by definition is reactive, I advise trying to avoid the need for a comeback by preempting the attack. Use what I called in my political consultant days an "inoculation spot." You start out by dissing yourself, which shows you're in control and in charge.

As Carrie Fisher says, once you make it a story, once you make it funny, you've rendered it harmless. So the question is, when should you dis yourself? Easy answer: when you've done something so incomprehensibly stupid, when the whole world knows it or when the embarrassing thing you've done is registering in everyone's mind the minute you walk into a room. It lances the boil, it lets the tension out of the room, and it lets everyone know that you know you're a screw-up and can handle it.

Last September a weepy Kentucky governor named Paul Patton lied about having an affair, then went on TV and admitted it. I'm not sure a joke would have helped—but blubbering like an idiot at the press conference certainly didn't impress the voters. How much worse damage could he have done if he had come out and said, "At least I didn't use a cigar"?

> CELEBRITY EXAMPLE: Paul Reubens (aka Pee-wee Herman) was on the MTV Video Music Awards after his arrest on lewdness charges at a movie theater. He walked onstage, looked at the audience, and said, "Heard any good jokes lately?" It brought the house down and gave him instant control over the situation.

Winona Ryder went on *Saturday Night Live* to make fun of her shoplifting arrest. In retrospect, probably not a good idea to do *before* her trial.

These are examples of avoiding the need for a withering comeback by essentially falling on your own comedy sword. But most of the time, you will not be a public figure needing to launch a preemptive strike. Instead, you will be the average Jane or Joe who wants a withering comeback to react to something rude someone said to you. Whether it came from a temporarily ignorant friend or a brutal foe, you want a knockout punch.

MY ALL-TIME-FAVORITE RESPONSE

Lady Astor once said to Winston Churchill, "If I were your wife I'd give you poison." Churchill's instant reply: "If I were your husband I'd drink it."

> SITUATION: You're in a bar. You politely, in a nonstalker way, try to meet a girl sitting with her friends and she says, "Get lost, creep."

> WRONG RESPONSE: Calling her a frigid bitch, a dyke, or throwing a beer in her face only proves that what she said is true, you are a creep.

> BETTER COMEBACKS:
> - *"Is that you or the freshman fifteen talking?"*
> - *"But not as creepy as the guy you'll probably end up with in a loveless trailer-park marriage."*
> - *"This is the last time I ever try to be nice to the homeless."*
> - *"Are you a model—you know, the before picture?"*
> - *"So how are things in Loch Ness?"* (a Joan Rivers line *from* Curb Your Enthusiasm)

SITUATION: You're at a business meeting, in a conference with your peers. You make a suggestion and an asshole coworker says, in an effort to torpedo you, "That is the dumbest idea I ever heard."

WRONG RESPONSE: Gunfire.

BETTER COMEBACKS:
- *"I know that's not you, that's just the liquor talking."*
- *"I don't know why you'd say that, I stole the idea from you."*
- *"I'm sure you said the same thing at your last five jobs."*

SITUATION: You're losing your hair and someone remarks on it.

WRONG RESPONSE: Don't use one of those old pithy sayings like "Grass doesn't grow on a busy street" or that baldness is a sign of a strong sex drive. They are too easily turned around. Instead, deal from a position of strength.

BETTER COMEBACKS:
- *"It's from stress, the stress of being near idiots like you."*
- *(rub head) "I like being bald—it feels like your wife's ass. Here, the rest of the guys know what I mean, here, rub and see if it feels like Cindy."*

- *"It just shows how God is unfair. I'm going bald and your ears and nose are the Amazon rain forest."*

SITUATION: You're out to dinner, the other couple you are with wants to stay out, you want to go home, they call you an old fart.

WRONG REPONSE: Dozing off.

BETTER COMEBACKS:
- *"Look, I lied, I'm not tired, it's just tough for me to hold up two ends of a conversation."*
- *"I have an excuse. I was up all night running from my parish priest."*
- *"So I assume you want to help the elderly and pick up the check."*

SITUATION: You're an overweight woman and you overhear a rude salesgirl say how immense you are.

WRONG RESPONSE: Weeping, threatening a lawsuit, or sending out for pizza.

BETTER COMEBACKS:
- *"Watch out, honey, or we're going to picket your house in the million-pound march."*

- *"I weigh 180 and if I had your brain, I'd weigh 180 pounds, 1 ounce."*
- *"What a coincidence, my weight is more than your college board score."*

So, in giving a withering comeback, you have to be ready to use all the tools at your disposal. You need to be observant, you need to listen to what the other person says, you need to be ready to pounce with an analogy, a topical reference, sarcasm, or a snap.

So as you prepare to graduate from Comeback 101, here are the rules:

1. *Turn it around and sell it as a strength.*

2. *Give a clever, off-the-point twist.*

3. *Slam them back by tying it to something near and dear to them.*

4. *Don't answer on the turf they set up, change it to another field of battle.*

5. *Go for the jugular.*

6.

When Not to Be
Funny/What's Not Funny

"Comedy = tragedy plus distance." I believe that was said by John Wilkes Booth.

1. *There are some things that are just not very funny . . . old jokes, forwarding bad, predictable e-mails, the rule of making fun of dead people too soon, otherwise known as the Abraham Lincoln rule.*

2. *There are things that are never, ever remotely funny for a civilian.**

---

* Doctors and nurses (noncivilians) in the ER use gallows humor to handle horribly tragic circumstances. If these things are said in public or are overheard by other civilians, they cause slapped faces and lawsuits.

- *Racial and ethnic humor. Take the advice of George Schlatter on this one: "Don't try and be Don Rickles. Even Don can't get away with it anymore."*
- *Disasters involving your own countrymen*
- *Horribly deformed children*
- *The deaths of beloved people*
- *9/11*
- *Child molesting*

3. *And there are things that, given the time since (distance from) the event and who you are, can be screamingly funny.*

EXAMPLE: At a recent benefit featuring Christopher Reeve, Robin Williams was taking pledges. He stood up, walked over to Christopher, and said, "And for just five thousand dollars more, watch him move his finger."

Robin could get away with it because 1) he's Robin, 2) he's a longtime friend of Christopher, and 3) the audience, after a long night of speeches about heroism, was ready to laugh.

Christopher Reeve himself tells a joke—"What's the difference between me and O.J.? O.J. walked." He can get away with it because he's Christopher Reeve, there's enough distance from the event to make it possibly funny, and what he said wasn't targeting himself.

So let's sum up how you can avoid trouble.

- *Be original and fresh.*
- *Getting a great laugh is not worth the sexual harassment lawsuit. Be 100 percent sure who you are talking to.*
- *Remember the fine line between outrageously funny humor and really bad taste. If you work "blue," you will offend people, so as a civilian, err on the side of caution.*

What happens if you slip and say something really offensive? If you're Trent Lott you resign. If you're not, then do what I always do—blame your medication.

Epilogue

So that's it, your guide on how to be funny. For most of you, the most important section is the one on public speaking. For others, it may be the section on story-telling. For the more adventurous, it's the examples on how to be funny in everyday conversation. It takes work and practice. But whatever your level of interest, there's only one more bit of advice I can give you. Call up a friend right now and be funny.

ABOUT THE AUTHOR

JON MACKS, author of *Heaven Talks Back*, *From Soup to Nuts*, and *Fuhgeddaboutit*, is a writer for *The Tonight Show with Jay Leno*. He has also written for the Academy Awards with Billy Crystal, Whoopi Goldberg, and Steve Martin and is a writer on *Hollywood Squares*. He lives in Los Angeles with his wife and three children.